ADAM'S RIVER

THE MYSTERY OF THE
ADAMS RIVER
SOCKEYE

ADAM'S RIVER

THE MYSTERY OF THE ADAMS RIVER SOCKEYE

MARK HUME

Photographs by
RICK BLACKLAWS

New Star Books
Vancouver
1994

For Maggie and Carol

Published by New Star Books Ltd., 2504 York Avenue, Vancouver, B.C., Canada V6K 1E3.
All rights reserved. No part of this work may be reproduced or used in any form or by any means — graphic, electronic, or mechanical — without the prior written permission of New Star Books. Any request for photocopying or other reprographic copying must be sent in writing to the Canadian Reprography Collective (Cancopy), 312 - 214 King Street West, Toronto, Ont. M5H 2S6.

Publication of this book is made possible by grants from the Canada Council, the Canadian Heritage Book Publishing Industry Development Program, and the Cultural Services Branch, Province of British Columbia.

Designed by Tom Moore
Printed and bound in Canada by Kromar Printing
1 2 3 4 5   98 97 96 95 94
First printing, August 1994

Canadian Cataloguing in Publication Data
Hume, Mark, 1950-
    Adam's river
    Includes bibliographical references and index.
    ISBN 0-921586-34-5
    1. Sockeye salmon — British Columbia — Adams River.
2. Adams River (B.C.)   I. Blacklaws, Richard William.   II. Title.
QL638.S2H85 1994   597'.55   C94-910517-1

CONTENTS

FOREWORD
THE RIVER SPIRIT

Some years ago I taught elementary school children on the wet coastal islands and in the dry interior plateau of British Columbia. When I moved on to develop curriculum for these children, I sought some common theme to which they could all relate. It was then that I realized that salmon are the single great unifying resource of our province. In this realization I understood that the word *resource* doesn't do them justice; salmon are the unifying *spirit* of all the Pacific drainage of British Columbia.

This should hardly have been a revelation to me, as I grew up on the banks of Vancouver Island's Campbell River where all six species of salmon spawned. I grew up in a house in which salmon was often the main course at dinner and even more often the main topic of dinner table conversation.

We talked of catching salmon of course, but we also talked of finding a gravel bar in which falling water levels had trapped salmon fry in a shallow pool of water. As children we told proudly how we scooped the fry back into the main stream. We told our parents of a valiant coho caught trying to make its way through a beaver dam into a little tributary creek.

Those were the natural forces that affected the salmon. We also heard about the unnatural and, at our table, un-Godly threats to the salmon, chief of which were hydroelectric dams. We heard about the death of the Columbia River salmon runs, destroyed by a diabolical alliance of the builders of concrete dams and concrete fish hatcheries that their supporters claimed would render the natural river obsolete.

This was the talk and fabric of my childhood, which I thought was somehow restricted to the Campbell River and my particular family's values. It was only in later years, when I went commercial fishing on a Kwakiutl-skippered seine boat, that I came to appreciate more fully the total dependence of our coast's culture on the salmon. When a seven-pound Fraser River-bound sockeye made its characteristic jump, coming clear of the water and then sliding on its side as it returned to its element, my skipper and father-in-law Herb

Assu came alive. This was not just with the anticipation of the catch, but with a deep spiritual conviction that all was right with the world. The spirituality was founded on the relationship that had existed between his ancestors and the ancestors of that salmon for thousands of years. It was given expression in the wonderful variety of salmon meals that my mother-in-law Leoda Assu made with the rich red flesh of these beautiful fish. Over the decade I spent on the seiner with Herb, a little of what was his became mine.

I was still spending summers on the seiner when I moved to the Chilcotin to teach school. I watched people dip-net the same salmon that I had seined for earlier in the month. I watched them cut and dry their catch just as we had canned our catch on the coast. I shared meals of interior salmon with the Chilcotin people. The texture of the familiar was now changed. The salmon had used much of its rich store of body oil by the time it got to the Chilcotin, but the spirituality of the food remained.

As on the coast, many of the old stories were of salmon. Chilcotin elder George Myers told me the story of Salmon Boy. The story tells of a boy who drifted to the sea one spring on a chunk of ice and then came back up-river in fall time with the salmon. When next I made the 400-mile drive to Vancouver, down along the glacial turquoise Chilcotin and the mud brown Fraser, I stopped to look at the churning waters from every viewpoint. I tried to imagine the boy, floating down on his ice floe. It seemed incredible, impossible. The ice would melt, the boy would drown, it would take too long. Then I tried to imagine the boy as a fish swimming upstream. Swimming up through the wild turbulence of the Fraser Canyon, finding the turn-off to the Chilcotin River. Then I began to understand incredible. That seven-pound fish that I had caught in Johnstone Strait not only had the reserves of fat to make this daunting journey, but it also had the imprinted spirit of a thousand life cycles and more, tracing and retracing familiar routes but always for the first and only time in their individual lives.

In the story of Salmon Boy, the people of this land and the salmon of our seas and rivers share a common spirit. The salmon moving up and down the Fraser and out to the farthest reaches of that great river's tributaries give life to this piece of the world in the way that nervous pulses up and down our backbone and out to the farthest reaches of our arms and legs give life to our bodies. It is the salmon that express the force of our land. Without the salmon, the land and the rivers would only survive as a corpse survives the death of the nervous system and the departure of the spirit.

Contemporary science identifies six species of sea-run salmon in British Columbia: chinook, coho, pink, chum, sockeye, and steelhead. Some rainbow and cutthroat trout also go to sea. Each species has many distinct stocks that will return home to a particular river or stream. Scientists believe that at one time there were somewhere in the neighborhood of 10,000 genetically unique stocks.

I suppose one of these stocks was the Elm Street coho stock that spawned in a ditch beside the school where I went to Grade 1. Around the time I was in Grade 5, the city of Campbell River "improved" Elm Street; workmen laid a big pipe in the ditch and filled it over. Last time I was in Campbell River, I looked along the now very busy Elm Street with its curbs, sidewalks and street lights and saw no sign of the creek anywhere. In the loss of that creek and its coho stock, we all lose a little of our spirit.

In this book we visit, or revisit, the places of the Adams sockeye. We move with them from the green waters of Johnstone Strait, through the rich browns of the Fraser Canyon, to the clarity of the Thompson as they make that first and final return to the Adams. The color and richness of this world are contained in Rick Blacklaws' photographs, along with images of the people who the sockeye feed and support along their migratory route.

In his text, Mark Hume tells about the loss of spirit that we suffered with the tragic loss of the great sockeye stocks from the Upper Adams and Salmon rivers — a loss of our spirit that diminishes us all. At the same time, the central story of this book is a tale of survival: the survival of Salmon Boy fighting his way back up rivers against the insane destruction caused by mindless empire builders at Hell's Gate in 1913. The nearness in time of this disaster to the devastation of World War I is not entirely coincidence. The twentieth century has been hard on people and fish around the world, but through all of these harsh times some sockeye have continued to find their way up the Fraser to the Thompson and up the Thompson to Shuswap Lake and through the lake to the Adams River.

I have been to the Salute to the Sockeye ceremonies that are held at the Adams River to recognize the beauty and wonder of the returning sockeye runs. I have stood on the banks, looking at the massed red fish and listening to the awe in the children's voices as they ask the questions that children will ask. There, as perhaps nowhere else, have I felt at one with the spirit of this land and its people — for that spirit is kept in the salmon.

Alan Haig-Brown
March 1994

ADAM'S RIVER

CHAPTER ONE
THE END OF THE
BEGINNING

The salmon has been resting in the pool for so long that silt has settled on its back. Its pectoral fins, which are normally used to trim the balance of the salmon as it moves through the water, are braced against the sandy bottom like the hands of a swimmer. The tip of the red hump, which suddenly formed just ahead of its dorsal fin a few weeks ago, is breaking the surface. The hump stamps it as a male spawner and makes it more vulnerable to predation by bears.

The salmon's eyes, which once measured sunlight over the North Pacific, triggering the migration home, are as golden as the fall leaves that litter the beach in front of it. They may be the last thing it sees, for the great journey is all but over.

His jaw is white; his head moss green. His skin, where free nerve endings receive the stimuli of touch and temperature and special glands extrude mucus to protect him, has changed from the luminescent blue of the ocean to a vibrant red. That skin, brown and marked with dark bars, camouflaged him during his first year as a fry in the nursery lake below the river, then transformed to the color of the sea and sky to hide him in the Pacific. Finally, in the last weeks of life, it turned the color of flames, flagging him as a sockeye for all the world to see, but more to the point, sending visual signals to the other salmon that he was ready to spawn.

As he awaits death he is gasping air. When he gapes, his nose comes out of the water, showing the small dark holes through which he found the trail to the Adams River. It was scent that led him through the silty Fraser and up the South Thompson, across Little Shuswap Lake and thus home, by an ancient route, to the reach of the river he was spawned in four years earlier. The proposition that salmon returned to the streams of their birth was, up until the early 1970s, dismissed by many fishery scientists as a preposterous theory. But a few of them, those who spent a lot of time on the rivers and saw what was happening, believed in the miracle. And eventually they proved that salmon have such a refined sense of smell they not only find their natal streams, but they can locate the patch of gravel they first emerged from. The characteristic smell of the river is imprinted on a fish at the earliest stages of life, but how that memory is retained is a mystery.

The proposition that salmon returned to the streams of their birth was, up until the early 1970s, dismissed by many fishery scientists as a preposterous theory.

Salmon smell using sacs inside the snout that sample water drawn into the chamber. The cells are wired directly to the forebrain. Scientists believe the organs of scent, known as olfactory glands, have not changed in thousands, perhaps millions of years, because they operate so perfectly. Sever the olfactory nerves — or plug the nose holes with cotton, as one scientist did — and a salmon will swim blindly past its stream of origin, just as if some internal guidance system had been erased.

There is more at work than a powerful sense of smell, however, for salmon often make route choices when they are far at sea, well beyond the scent of their home rivers. Scientists don't understand exactly how it works, but they know that salmon use a measurement of light to determine the timing of their migration, and that they can detect the earth's magnetic field. Some also think the fish align themselves along weak electrical currents that flow through the ocean, thereby finding their way upstream or downstream through the conflicting tides of the Pacific.

In the world of fishes, the migration of salmon stands out as an epic journey that is complex and difficult. Yet if you crack open the skull of a salmon you will find this: a small, grayish brain the size of a peanut. It's not impressive, and it is hard to imagine it as the command centre for a fantastically complicated navigation system.

So how do they do it? How do they find their way to the ocean, cross thousands of kilometers of apparently featureless sea, and return again on cue? That puzzle is still being pieced together, but in a general sense the answer is found in the way a salmon uses its entire body as a sensory organ — responding to light, atmospheric pressure, temperature, salinity and scent.

Sockeye at rest.

There are several finely tuned sensory nerves in a salmon, perhaps the most notable being the vagus nerve, a large mixed complex with several branches, including the body lateral line. The lateral line, so distinctive it seems to divide the fish in half, top from bottom, responds to displacement of water and pressure. It is connected to the fish's acoustics system (which includes an inner ear, but no middle or outer ear) so the fish can sense sound as well as hear it. There are nerves that function as temperature receptors and others that receive electrical impulses. And there are some nerves that have unknown functions.

With its array of sensory receptors, a salmon is remarkably attuned to its environment. Beyond that, its secret is encoded in the mysteriously intricate world of genetics. The salmon has, it seems, inherited powers and behavioral traits that reach back to a time when the earth was much younger.

Salmoniformes, the great family of fishes to which sockeye belong, are known from the Cretaceous era, a period marked by the birth of the Rockies and the death

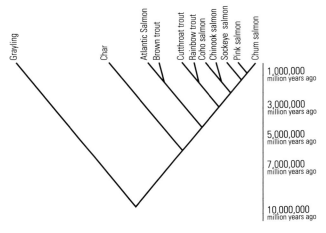

Grayling · Char · Atlantic Salmon · Brown trout · Cutthroat trout · Rainbow trout · Coho salmon · Chinook salmon · Sockeye salmon · Pink salmon · Chum salmon

1,000,000 million years ago

3,000,000 million years ago

5,000,000 million years ago

7,000,000 million years ago

10,000,000 million years ago

It is believed that salmon evolved from a trout stock, becaming distinct species within the last 4 million years. Sockeye probably speciated about 1.5 million years ago. Biologists have recently classifed steelhead as the sixth species of Pacific salmon.

of the last dinosaurs, that began about 135 million years ago as the Jurassic epoch was ending.

The oldest known fossil salmonid, *Eosalmodrift-woodensis*, was found in Eocene freshwater lake sediments, which date back 55 million years. Extinct forms of Pacific salmon, closely related to sockeye (*Oncorhynchus nerka*), have been found in Miocene deposits 30 million years old.

One of the prehistoric salmon was a spectacular fish that measured 1.9 meters and had enormous breeding teeth. It is known as the *Smilodonichthys rastrosus*. The Smilodon probably behaved much like today's sockeye, feeding in large interior lakes or the ocean and returning to rivers to spawn. Nobody knows why this fearsome salmon vanished and the much smaller sockeye, which lived at the same time, survived.

Because it spends one quarter of its four-year life in freshwater, the sockeye is tied more closely to its place of origin and therefore considered among the most primitive of the Pacific salmon species. Pink and chum, on the other hand, run immediately to the sea after hatching and so are believed to be more highly evolved. Some biologists, however, argue that the reverse is true; that salmon originated in saltwater, and therefore pink or chum are the most primitive and sockeye the most developed. However you look at it, salmon are ancient creatures.

Genetic studies show close similarity between rainbow and cutthroat trout, coho and chinook — and between pink and sockeye salmon. All of the family members are characterized by, among other things, a large proportion of cartilage in the cranium. They are tough-headed fishes. Although the reason for that isn't known, the explanation may lie right here, in the glacial bed of the Adams, which young salmon swim through as if it were water. Salmon start their life in the gravel — and that is where they end it, if they live long enough to spawn.

The silt that settled on the back of the male fish I encountered one October afternoon had been stirred up by females digging nests upstream. Each female fish builds a cluster of several nests, collectively known as a redd. The male would have lain close to one of the females, fighting off rivals and at times arcing his body in an action that mimicked her digging action.

After he had spawned with her in each of the nests, he slipped away to die, while she stayed to guard the redd as long as she could. You will often find the males along the Adams in the fall, lying in quiet water like this, awaiting death. If you approach slowly, they will let you get close, perhaps even within touching distance. The male I found was nosed up against a fan of sand near a beaver dam. In a side channel, coho salmon fry from the year before darted among the twigs. One bright fish was swimming in tight spirals, each twist creating a silver flash. Its erratic behavior indicated that it too was dying, but without having ever known the sea.

On a nearby gravel bar, gulls were resting, waiting for a meal to float to them. They would eat the eyes first.

The sockeye's tail, which had been moving since he emerged from the gravel four years ago, continued to wave rhythmically in the current as I knelt in the sand to watch.

One of the miracles of fish such as this is that, because of a layer of fatigue-free muscle — called "red" muscles — that beats like a metronome, they never tire from steady swimming. Until the end. And when they do stop swimming, they cease existing.

A salmon's body is made up of muscle blocks separated by connective tissue. There are three layers of muscles: white, pink and red. Along the sides, just under the skin, lie lateral muscles which are well-supplied with blood vessels, have a high fat content, and are known as the "red" muscles, because they are dark in color. The red muscles are used in steady, untiring swimming activity.

The question of how fish generate so much speed with bodies that contain so little power continues to confound scientists. A formula, known as Gray's paradox,

Main entrée at the Adams River estuary — seagulls feast on dying sockeye.

shows it is mathematically impossible for fish to swim as fast as they do. Engineers, hoping to come up with new, super-efficient designs for submarines, have been chipping away at the problem for years. Recent experiments have shown that most of the locomotive power of a fish comes from the area of red muscle nearest the tail, but the still-unsolved puzzle is a reminder that there are forces at work in nature that are beyond our comprehension. We may never understand some of them.

As evening falls the sockeye's tail loses its beat. It lies motionless for a moment, struggles to regain momentum, then quits again. Finally he drifts back slowly from the shore and starts to sink into darker water. His fins are worn; bacteria attack his once beautiful skin. The current catches him, turns him over, the white belly up now for the first time in his existence. The river carries him down towards the lake. It is not all over. Not quite yet. Locked in his body are nutrients, gathered from the sea, that will slowly be released to feed the microscopic organisms that feed the small fish that will soon emerge to replace him.

As he drifts, eyes clouded, receptor nerves now dead to the sense of bursting life in the river, he passes over spawning nests dug in the gravel. The redds are visible ovals of clean gravel where the silt and algae have been swept away by a female salmon, repeatedly arcing her body against the bottom. One of the redds holds the eggs he fertilized, his sperm swimming as wildly as seeds blown by the wind.

The sockeye of the Adams River spawn in early October, arriving back at their home river with a punctuality that is fascinating. Chinook, coho and pink salmon also spawn in the Adams, but the species don't interbreed. At first glance the salmon types may look similar, but there are great differences in appearance, timing of their runs, and in their life histories.

Even if all you had to go on were the eggs, a trained eye could tell which belonged to the sockeye because they are a much darker orange-red than the paler chinook and more opaque coho eggs. The sockeye eggs are also smaller. Sockeye carry more eggs for their size than any of the other salmon, having roughly 3,000 to 4,000 while a coho might have 2,600, a chinook less than 2,000 and a pink 1,200 to 1,900. The fertility of salmon varies from one river to the next and increases with the size of the female. Compared to other fish, salmon do not produce a lot of eggs — but the eggs are relatively enormous, generally 6 to 8 millimeters in diameter, allowing fry to live for long periods on the large yolk sacs.

A big female will carry more eggs than a small one, and scientists believe the mix of sizes among the salmon in a river is a "survival strategy" that has evolved to take full advantage of the diverse habitat.

KOKANEE

Kokanee are sockeye salmon that remain throughout their lives in freshwater. Except for their small size (mean lengths from 18 to 30 cm), kokanee look like sockeye, even taking on the distinctive red body and green head coloration at spawning time. It is believed that kokanee diverted from sockeye stocks in recent geological times. In some cases kokanee are found in the same lakes used by sockeye, but in many instances they are found in waters that don't contain sockeye.

Whenever a stream changes direction, a pool forms at the bend because of spiraling water circulation. The water scours the bottom and shifts gravel downstream until the current slows and the gravel settles out, forming bars. The coarser material is deposited first, followed by finer material, which is dropped along the bar where currents are slower. As a result, all spawning gravel is not created equal in a given pool.

A small female might be pushed off the best spawning gravel by a bigger sockeye, but her smaller eggs, because they require less oxygen, can successfully incubate in poorer quality gravel in slower water.

If the water flow is not just right, the eggs will die from lack of oxygen, or they will freeze, or get crushed by drifting ice. That is why the sockeye chose this place, downstream from the big, blue depths of Adams Lake: because it is perfect.

Sockeye are more diverse than any of the other Pacific salmon in their ability to adapt to a wide range of spawning habitat. Small ponds, spring-fed creeks and lake margins are all used by sockeye to spawn. But the heaviest concentration is found in rivers like the Adams that run from big lakes, because they provide a stable flow of water.

The nests are typically placed to take advantage of a good flow of oxygenated water and are dug in a way that creates a back eddy in the current, increasing the percolation of water through the gravel.

The eggs contain a completely balanced diet of proteins, carbohydrates, vitamins and minerals. The vitelline vein, which runs through the centre of the egg sac, picks up oxygen from the water and delivers it to the developing salmon.

About a month after the eggs have been deposited in a shallow nest and buried with a protective covering of gravel, they show the first signs of life. Dark eye spots form and slowly start to grow. If the water flow is not just right the eggs will die from lack of oxygen, or they will freeze, or get crushed by drifting ice. But that is why the sockeye chose this place, downstream from the big, blue depths of Adams Lake: because it is perfect.

The river meanders back and forth, snaking gently through the valley, creating pools and gravel bars as it goes. There are fast runs of shallow water known as riffles, deep pools in rocky canyons, and quiet back channels of calm water.

Rainwater brings nitrogen and carbon dioxide to the river, picking up hydrogen, oxygen, sulfur, phosphorus, magnesium, potassium and iron as it runs across the forest floor, dissolving the substances as it goes.

Studies have shown that the litter in a deciduous woodland liberates some 6 million calories per square meter; enough energy to feed a human for 2.5 days. How much of this energy is moved into the stream is not known, but it is clear the health and productivity of a river is directly related to the environment surrounding it.

The nutrients brought by the runoff, together with the massive phosphorus and nitrogen loading that decomposing salmon release, feed algae, phytoplankton, insects and rooted aquatic plants. The minute food sources are vital to the survival of the young salmon. And the water quality itself, particularly the oxygen content, will determine whether the eggs survive to hatch.

The Adams River, unlike many salmon rivers in British Columbia, is protected in its entirety. Roderick Haig-Brown Provincial Park, a 988-hectare preserve of Douglas fir, cottonwood, birch, alder, ponderosa pine, hemlock and cedar, buffers both sides of the river from its source, at Adams Lake, to its outlet at Shuswap Lake, 11 kilometers downstream.

Some of the trees along the river show signs of having once been stripped of bark by the ancestors of Shuswap Indians. The remains of ancient winter residences known as pithouses, and the continuing use of the adjacent Quaaout, Hustalen and Toop Indian reserves testify to the long relationship the Shuswap people have had with the Adams. There are village sites that date back 6,000 years and there is ample evidence a rich and complex culture flourished here because of the sockeye runs.

In 1977 Bill Brown and Greta Lundborg surveyed the valley for the provincial archaeologist's office, finding evidence of native communities at the mouth of the river and at its outlet on Adams Lake. The winter village at the head of the river, located just outside the park on the Hustalen Reserve, was spread over 15,000 square meters. It was described by the archaeologists as "spectacular" and must have been an amazing sight at the height of its use. Dozens of winter houses, each built to accommodate about 25 people, would have been strung out along the flat, grassy bench on the lakeshore. The houses were dug into the earth and then covered with a roof of bark, moss and dirt supported by a wooden framework. There were usually two entrances; one coming down through the roof on a ladder and another side entrance for use by women. Nearby were bark-lined pits where surplus food was stored. There would have been racks where strips of orange-fleshed salmon were hung to smoke or dry in the wind. In addition to netting and spearing salmon, the Indians hunted deer, bear, beaver, geese, ducks and mountain sheep. They collected over 135 species of local plants including lamb's quarter leaf, Indian rhubarb stalk, rose hip, hazelnut, Spanish moss and a tobacco-like plant, kinnikinnik, that was cultivated and smoked in tubular soapstone pipes.

At the river mouth, on the Quaaout Reserve, the researchers found another village. Along the river itself there were no villages.

"I think you will find that each family had their own little place all up and down the river," Chief Harvey Jewels of the Adams Lake Band told the archaeologists

There are rock paintings hidden away on cliff faces, and in many places beside the trails you can see the obvious rectangular depressions left by old winter houses.

before they began their work. And that's just what they did find: small, scattered groupings of houses.

In addition to the winter camps, Brown and Lundborg also recorded a remarkable site in the canyon area, midway up the river. There, where the river passes through towering granitic greenstone walls, they found a fishing place of immense importance, where people from both villages may have gathered in the fall.

"Spawning salmon gathered in the quiet waters of the canyon mouth before negotiating the torrent," the researchers reported. "Once in the gorge, they rested in small, still pools hewn from the solid rock of the canyon wall by the action of the back eddies. The harvest of fish from these waters must have been bountiful indeed, judging from the 365 storage cellars excavated in the terraces above the gorge." The cache pits were small circular depressions in the earth that would have been lined with bark and filled with smoked or dried salmon. Treated properly, the fish would keep for several months, feeding the family throughout the winter.

The Adams River at Shuswap Lake.

There are rock paintings hidden away on cliff faces, and in many places beside the trails you can see the obvious rectangular depressions left by old winter houses.

The turbulent waters of the canyon area along the Adams River.

(It is illegal to tamper with any of these sites. Because of fears about vandalism, no effort is made in the park to draw the attention of tourists to the heritage sites.)

The salmon run is still an important part of the Shuswap peoples' lives — and of their economy. The resort hotel built on the Quaaout Reserve, on Little Shuswap Lake, is a modern way of tying in to the sockeye run. In the past, natives would have been spearing salmon and using the dried fish as a trade commodity. Today they turn the salmon into profit by catering, at least in the fall, to tourists who are drawn by the global fame of the Adams River run.

For 10,000 years there was little human impact on the river's salmon. But when the area was settled by Europeans in the early 1900s, logging started and the forests in the watershed were soon cut down. Immense damage was done to the salmon run. The timber in the valley is now mostly second growth and the environment has stabilized, but careless logging or mining, especially up tributaries like Nikwikwaia (Gold) and Hiuihill (Bear) creeks, could again threaten the Adams, despite the buffering nature of Haig-Brown Park. When hillsides are torn up by poor roadbuilding or the cross-yarding of timber, rain carries heavy loads of silt into small streams that in turn tumble into the main river. The silt, which can travel a long way from its source, settles out on gravel beds, suffocating salmon nests by cutting off the flow of oxygen. Park designation marks the Adams as a special river, but provides protection only to the land immediately surrounding the river. Most of the vast watershed that sustains the system remains vulnerable.

More than 19 million sockeye have spawned in the Adams since 1953, which averages out to about 460,000 a year or 42,000 a kilometer. In reality it doesn't work out that neatly. Sockeye return on a four-year cycle, and every fourth year is a dominant run, with about 2 million salmon returning to spawn and another 8 million being taken by the commercial fishery. The run is substantially smaller in intervening years, sometimes dropping to only a few thousand fish.

Unlike many species of fish, including steelhead and Atlantic salmon which can reproduce more than once, sockeye die soon after spawning. That means they get just one chance at it, so they must make all the right choices if they are to survive as a species. Their epic journey of migration from the sea is made because they instinctively know this place works for them. It has a good winter flow of water; strong enough to keep the gravel clean and push oxygen down to the incubating eggs, but not so powerful it scours out the nests. And the temperature is optimal, allowing the young salmon to emerge at a time when the lake below is rich with nutrients.

During the winter, with snow blanketing the heavily forested hills around the watershed, the river is at its lowest. It drops from a mean flow of about 40 cubic meters per second (cms) in October and November, to 17 cms in February, burbling along under the ice. It starts to build again rapidly in the spring, and when the salmon emerge it helps push them down to the nursery lakes, Little Shuswap and Shuswap.

With cold air draining down the valley of Nikwikwaia Creek, the Adams River corridor is slightly cooler than surrounding areas. At Chase there are 145 frost-free days in a typical year, while there are 134 at Adams Lake — and 90 along the

RODERICK HAIG-BROWN

Roderick Langmere Haig-Brown (1908-1976) was a conservationist, angler and writer. His books on fishing are considered angling classics. From 1972 to 1976, Haig-Brown was director of the Nature Trust in B.C., a private organization that works to conserve ecologically significant areas. The Nature Trust owns 46 hectares along the Adams River which it has leased to the provincial government as part of the 988-hectare Roderick Haig-Brown Provincial Park.

Emerging from their gravel nests, the young salmon are at first nourished by egg sacs, which are slowly absorbed. Trout and other predators feed on the swarms of young fish.

banks of the river. Mid-winter finds the valley blanketed by snow, and the river murmuring gently under a covering of ice.

But even in the stillness of December there is a proliferation of life along the river that is tied in to the salmon run. In the snow you will see a flurry of animal tracks left by coyotes, mink, otter and mice. The tracks of dogs are easy enough to sort out for, like those left by humans, they seem to weave pointlessly back and forth, stopping at everything of interest and little of importance. The wild tracks, however, run straight and true, from cover to cover, then out of the trees and across the snowy gravel bars. Follow them, and at the end you'll find diggings — and underneath it all, the carcass of a salmon, preserved in the snow. Ravens come down to feed after the salmon diggers have gone. And an eagle might drop in, not too proud to feed on the carrion.

In February, when the flow of the river is at its lowest, the eggs hatch into tiny creatures called alevins, which look about as much like a salmon as a tadpole looks like a frog. The alevins are transparent little things with goggly eyes, fins like spun glass, and an orange yolk sac loaded with nutrients distending their bellies.

The eggs don't all hatch at the same time. Often the lower eggs in the nest hatch first because the water percolating up through the gravel is slightly warmer. The timing of the hatch is determined by the temperature and if it is a long cold winter, the alevins will emerge later in the spring.

For the next three months the alevins live off the nutrients in the egg sac. They stay in the gravel, for the first month burrowing deep beneath the level of their nests, remaining hidden from the predatory world above them and (maybe this is why they have such tough heads) darting through the crevasses in the loose river bottom. What by daylight appears to be a fishless pool may in fact contain millions of tiny alevins, holding in the gravel where sunlight cannot penetrate. During this period the young sockeye are so sensitive to light they will dive deep into the gravel to avoid it. Scientists describe the fish as being "extremely negatively phototactic." In one experiment 50 sockeye alevins were kept in a constantly lit gravel tank. None emerged; they all died of starvation rather than emerging to face the light.

The death rate during the first stage of life is immense, as insects and small fish known as sculpins, or bullheads, burrow into the gravel searching for eggs or alevins. Mink, birds and other predators may dig them out as well. A mortality rate of 90 percent from egg to fry is not uncommon — and neither is it alarming. Salmon, as do all fishes, produce a great surplus of eggs and young.

"Fishes are well known for their high potential fecundity, with most species releasing thousands to millions of eggs annually. The world would be full of fish if the environment did not take its toll of eggs and hatched young," Carl Bond comments in his book *Biology of Fishes*.

In May and June — a timing that synchronises the salmon with enormous changes taking place in the lake below — the alevins emerge from the gravel with their egg sacs mostly absorbed. They are about 2.5 centimeters long and have brown, mottled backs. They emerge at night, so are seldom seen by people. But salmon researcher R.A. Banes stayed up to watch them, and has given a remarkably detailed description of the first movements of emerging sockeye. He reports how, in a series of attempts, the fish swim towards the surface, getting a few centimeters higher each time. They must achieve neutral buoyancy, and to do that they have to reach the surface to gulp air and fill their swim bladders. They swim more frantically now than at any other period in their lives, with their tails beating furiously and their bodies hanging perpendicular in the water. Reaching the surface, the fish cruise with their nose tips out, gulping air to fill their swim bladders. Repeated trips to the surface are needed before they gain neutral buoyancy and finally become horizontal in the water.

Almost immediately the fry begin to drift downstream to Shuswap Lake, where they will form into schools. Their arrival in the nursery lakes must be timed perfectly, for if they are not aligned with the plankton blooms that occur in the spring, they will not survive.

CHAPTER TWO

THE

LAKES

Teh current of the Little River is deceptive. Seen from the highway it seems a gentle flowing body of water, but when you are on it in a canoe you see how fast it is moving. Drop an anchor and you instantly feel the power of the river, shimmering over the great fan of gravel it has spilled at its outlet into Little Shuswap Lake.

When sockeye fry emerge from Adams River they drift down along the shore of Shuswap Lake to the mouth of the Little, where 300,000 sockeye spawn in a dominant year. The fry from both rivers flow down into Little Shuswap Lake, and remain there long enough to gain the strength they need to swim back up to Shuswap Lake, where they will reside for the next year.

The mouth of the Little is a good place to see fry making their entrance into the lake. And it is a good place to see trout and bats.

As evening falls and a coolness settles over the water, insects rise from the surface to dance over the river. That's when the bats come, fluttering down along the river to the lake. The bats are drawn by the same thing that draws the millions of young sockeye that are seen passing just beneath the surface in small glimmering schools — an abundant source of food.

In the quiet water just off the edge of the current, chironomids, tiny insects that resemble mosquitoes, are hatching. Sockeye fry dart after them, leaving dimples on the surface. In the air the bats swoop and dive as they feed on the adult chironomids. When dawn comes the bats retreat to the darkness of their nests and the salmon sink into the depths, collecting in large schools along the lake margin.

Loons, mergansers and trout feed heavily on salmon fry. In one ten-year study of pink salmon, researchers found up to 86 percent of the fry were killed by other fish. And an experiment in New Brunswick showed that three to five times as many Atlantic salmon smolts survived when mergansers were removed from the area.

At river mouths in the spring, rainbow trout gather to wait for schools of fry. A rainbow swirls at a pod of sockeye, splashing on the surface, then is gone. With so many fry and the year-old smolts from last year still available to feed on, the trout are overwhelmed by choice. Scientists call this "predator swamping" and see it as a technique salmon use to survive heavy predation. After the trout are satiated and have sunk to the bottom to rest, the fry keep coming. It is nature's twist on the old saying, "Safety in numbers."

Biologists have found a close relationship between the trout populations of the Shuswap lakes and the Adams River salmon run. A year after a dominant run, the trout population booms. The reason is simple enough. In a dominant year the young trout have all the food they want, and they grow rapidly. In the subsequent years the trout population dwindles as its main food supply is reduced.

Rainbow trout from as far away as Spences Bridge, 150 kilometers south on the

An aerial view of Little Shuswap Lake looking east toward Shuswap Lake.

In the nursery lakes, salmon fry are part of an intricate food web. They feed on tiny diatoms, algae and phyto- plankton and on larger herbivorous insects such as mayflies. Feeding on the fish are predators such as loons and trout.

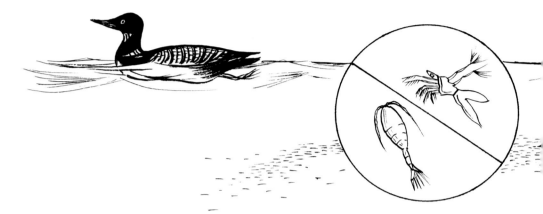

Thompson River, come to the Shuswap lakes to feed on fry. They follow the spawning salmon upriver to the mouth of the Adams, devouring loose eggs that tumble down with the current, and later taking the drifting flesh of rotting salmon carcasses. They seem to know instinctively that if they wait, salmon fry will issue forth by the millions from the river in the spring.

The trout, like the bats that dance above, a loon that swims nearby, and the thousands of tiny toads hatching on the riverbank, are part of a complex food web, at the centre of which lie the sockeye. At the base of it all are ancient organisms billions of years old — some of them so microscopic that they weren't discovered by scientists until the 1970s.

Unlike any of the other Pacific salmon species, sockeye rely heavily on nursery lakes to nurture their young. Some salmon, like pinks, migrate almost immediately to the ocean after emerging from the gravel. Others, like chinook, reside in a stream from a few weeks to a year or more. But sockeye live extensively in lakes. Typically an Adams River sockeye will stay in the Shuswap lakes for a year, feeding on small insects initially, then shifting to tiny plankton which flourish in the lakes, fed by the nitrogen and phosphorus from decomposing bodies of dead spawners.

Shuswap Lake covers about 30,000 hectares. The number of dead spawners per hectare of water ranges from less than one, following a weak run, to 68 in a dominant year. The level of salmon carcass fertilization that takes place directly determines the density of plankton in the lake, which in turn determines the survival rate of sockeye fry over the following year. The correlation has been proved in experiments in lakes throughout British Columbia, where the federal Department of Fisheries and Oceans has had spectacular luck enriching sockeye lakes with agricultural fertilizer.

John Stockner, the DFO limnologist who has led the lake fertilization work, says what he is really doing is replacing the nutrients that once naturally occurred when salmon runs were much bigger.

Several years ago Stockner did some bottom core sampling on a number of lakes. What he found when he analyzed the sediment was a clear line — marking the period when heavy commercial fishing began on the coast, and the number of spawners dropped dramatically.

Dead salmon are the fertilizer for plankton, which in turn feed the young sockeye. Managing the salmon harvest must now include a calculation as to how many salmon need to get back, not just to fill the spawning beds, but also to enrich the lakes.

For many years the commercial fishery took 94 percent of the run. And there was an upstream catch by natives and homesteaders on top of that. Some runs may have been fished into extinction. Today, on a healthy run like the Adams, the overall total catch can be as high as 80 percent, with four salmon taken for every one that gets through to the spawning beds.

Stockner's lake fertilization program mainly targets coastal lakes, fast-flushing bodies of water which are among the least productive in the world. The phosphorus and nitrate fertilizer is dusted onto the lakes by an aircraft. It's a lot like spraying crops, and it has a profound and immediate impact. When a test was run on Great Central Lake on Vancouver Island, the results were astonishing. Before fertilization the big, clear lake had a run of about 350,000 sockeye; after fertilization its stock of sockeye jumped to 750,000 fish.

In Shuswap Lake, dead salmon are the fertilizer, slowly releasing phosphorus and nitrogen in the fall, and then again in the spring after the thaw. Because of Stockner's research, the complexity of managing the salmon harvest must now include a calculation as to how many salmon need to get back, not just to fill the spawning beds, but also to enrich the lakes.

"We attempt to manage the runs so we get enough carcasses back to support the plankton," says Stockner.

S cientists have known about algae and plankton blooms for a long time. But because of their minute size, the much smaller nanoplankton and picoplankton that sockeye feed on weren't discovered until recently. The first hint of the microscopic organisms' existence came in the early 1950s when a Swedish scientist saw a cloudy green substance in the ice of lakes that were thought to be sterile. In 1977 "little round green things" were observed by biologists in some New Zealand lakes.

"It is true to say that the picoplankton lay mostly unseen or unrecognized in both lakes and oceans for several decades of scientific inquiry, until two oceanographic schools simultaneously announced their discovery of planktonic chroococcoid cyanobacteria [in 1979]," Stockner writes.

The following year the discovery was extended to European lakes, and to North America for the first time in 1984.

In the late 1970s, scientists began using the term picoplankton to describe the single-celled microorganisms. Slightly larger organisms are called nanoplankton, and up from that are phytoplankton.

It wasn't until the early 1980s, however, that scientists really began to explore the microscopic world of picoplankton and nanoplankton. The breakthrough came when a magnifying technique known as epifluorescence microscopy became available. To scientists like Stockner, it was a revelation, for below the minute world of phytoplankton a new, microscopic plain of life had suddenly opened up.

SALMON AND pH LEVELS

The term pH is used to indicate the relative alkalinity or acidity of water, in a range that goes from 0 to 14. The point of neutrality is pH 7. Above this the solution is alkaline and below it is acidic. Waters that are excessively acid or alkaline are not conducive to good growth and survival of salmon. The pH level in Shuswap Lake is 6.9 — ideal for salmon and the small plants and animals they feed on.

"Just as particle physicists in search of the ultimate form of matter discovered complexity instead of simplicity, and a strong interconnectedness among both living and nonliving matter, so also, within the present decade, aquatic microbiologists and ecologists, armed with new means of observation and measurement have discovered incredible complexity and interrelatedness in the realm of the minute life forms," he wrote.

Picoplanktons can either be free-living or attached to the cell surface of algae. The organisms are so small a picture of one had to be enlarged more than 100,000 times to make it the size of a dollar coin.

Using electron microscopy and treating picoplankton with electrolytic or fluorescein dyes, like alcian blue and fluoro bora, scientists have been able to produce photographs of microbic life too tiny to be seen by the naked eye. And, like most things seen under immense magnification, the organisms have fantastical shapes. One looks like a tiny golf ball with nodules all over it, another seems to be an old Russian sputnik that has come whirling in from deepest space, yet another looks like a sponge plucked from the ocean floor, and a picoplankton colony appears as an impressionistic canvas. It is incredible to realize that at the bottom of the food chain lies a vast, swirling sea of life that seems as if it were designed as much by Monet as by nature.

One picoplankton looks like a tiny golf ball with nodules all over it, another seems to be an old Russian sputnik that has come whirling in from deepest space.

It is not a stagnant world. Scientists have seen picoplankton inside larger phytoplankton — showing that even at that microscopic level there is predatory behavior. In Shuswap Lake, big fish eat little fish, little fish eat phytoplankton, and phytoplankton feed on the nanoplankton. Feeding the base of the food chain: decomposing salmon — nutrients from the sea.

Picoplankton communities in Shuswap Lake are extensive from the surface to a depth of 20 meters. Densities peak in August and September, and the communities flourish with increased phosphorus concentration which is flushed into the lake by spring runoff.

Sockeye fry are very effective at reducing plankton populations, and are capable of "grazing off" a crop so thoroughly that in the following year, fish have a harder time finding food.

In Quesnel Lake, for example, research has indicated that large smolts are produced by plankton popu-

lations built up after years of low grazing. Some scientists believe heavy grazing is a key factor in the cyclic dominance of sockeye runs. If it is, then a folding back of the food web occurs, in which the different layers become interwoven: the number of decomposing adults determines the number of smolts which in turn determines the number of adults a few years hence.

Rainbow trout, connoisseur of sockeye eggs, alevin and fry.

Stockner says sorting out the complexities of the relationship between sockeye and microscopic plankton is a major challenge. And it is an increasingly important one. Rapid urban and industrial growth is taking place throughout British Columbia and can be seen on the shores of the Shuswap lakes, where cottages, golf courses and retirement villages are springing up. If the health of our sockeye runs depends on the existence of organisms too tiny to even see, new questions must be raised about environmental standards. Simply put, how much can we degrade the quality of water in the Shuswap before the bottom literally drops out of the food chain, triggering a collapse in the salmon?

Estuary habitat at Adams River.

During the low temperatures and low light of winter the plankton crop in Shuswap Lake doesn't grow as rapidly, forcing sockeye fry to feed intermittently. At times they fast for weeks. Under the sun of spring, plankton again flourish, and the fry feed heavily as they prepare for their outmigration — a hazardous journey that will take them to the sea and force them to undergo some remarkable morphological and physiological changes.

As the newly emerged fry enter the lake from the Adams River, the year-old sockeye from the previous spawning, now called smolts, are beginning their exodus, out through Little Shuswap Lake, down the South Thompson and into the Fraser River.

The longer hours of daylight and higher temperatures trip a hormonal switch in the salmon, triggering body changes and starting the migration. Studies have found the migrations begin after spring water temperatures rise above 4.4°C; by the time the water is 10°C, most of the smolts have gone. They typically gather in large schools at the outlet of the lake before moving at night, *en masse*, into the river. It's unfortunate that places from which to view this movement aren't known, because it must be an incredible sight. At Lake Iliamna, in Alaska, researchers once watched as 270 million sockeye fry, weighing an estimated 2000 tons, moved into the river. The vast bulk migrated out of the lake over a four-hour period, leaving between 10 p.m. and 2 a.m. in an apparent effort to avoid predators.

Not all sockeye fry outmigrate in such a short time, however. Studies on Cultus Lake, in the Fraser Valley, found there was a slow buildup at first, with a small percentage of fry departing over a long period and 20 to 80 percent leaving in 5 to 15 days.

"On calm evenings following bright, warm days the surface of the outlet end of the lake would be literally alive with young sockeye jumping from or finning the surface, and the migrations after dark would be heavy," writes Russell Foerster, a federal fisheries expert who studied sockeye from 1924 to 1962. "On dull days, with or without rain, no sockeye would be seen at the surface and the night migration would drop off appreciably."

I t takes more than two years for water to circulate out of Shuswap Lake, so there is precious little current to guide the fish. How do they find the exit? Scientists believe they follow warm water that is pushed toward the river mouth by outflowing winds, and that they navigate along the shoreline, using visual clues. But there are also early signs of the sockeye's remarkable ability to use an internal compass and undertake celestial navigation. In their book *Pacific Salmon Life Histories*, Cornelis Groot and Leo Margolis write that in British Columbia's Babine Lake, "sockeye smolts apparently have direction-finding systems for locating the outlet that include sun-compass and polarized light cues. A shift to a non-celestial mode of orientation was indicated with increasing cloud cover, apparently cued by the earth's magnetic field."

Once they have begun their migration, the smolts show every sign of pursuing it with motivation. Rather than letting the current drift them along, they actively swim downstream. When they encounter rapids, as they do frequently on their trip towards Hell's Gate, on the Fraser River, they turn and pass through with their tails downstream, the way a drift boat does. It isn't known if the migration is continuous, day and night.

As they head to the sea, the salmon prepare themselves for a dramatic shift from freshwater to saltwater. They must become stronger swimmers, learn new methods for avoiding predators — and undergo physical changes so that the salt doesn't kill them.

The extent of the changes is seen in the alteration of their outward appearance. When they first enter the nursery lake they have a rounder shape and are covered with dark elliptical bars, known as parr marks, which help them hide in weed beds. As they embark on their great downstream journey, they become more streamlined and take on a glistening silver appearance. The most significant change is internal, however.

Fish take in water through permeable surfaces, primarily gills and skin. Because they are constantly submerged, there has to be a way to check the process — otherwise they would suffer what scientists refer to as "internal drowning." To keep from absorbing too much, freshwater fish have developed remarkably efficient pumping systems to drive unneeded water from their bodies via the kidneys, discharging volumes of dilute urine. In saltwater, fish lose water through the gills and skin, replacing it by drinking sea water that is in part absorbed through the gut. The higher the salinity, the greater the rate of drinking. Marine species commonly swallow sea water amounting to over 35 percent of their body weight each day.

In a miraculous transformation, Adams River sockeye adjust to the shock of saltwater by changing their "osmoregulatory mechanisms." Their skin, gills and internal organs such as the kidneys take on new roles as they move into saltwater.

The key to a salmon's ability to switch to saltwater lies in chloride-secreting cells it develops in its gills to get rid of excess salt. Some salmon, like chum which migrate to the ocean early in life, are ready to adapt from the outset. But other species apparently don't change until they are a year old. In one experiment both chum and coho fry were placed suddenly in saltwater. The chum survived the experiment, but the saltwater killed the coho.

Sockeye develop the chloride-secreting cells at some point before they reach the sea. The timing of the move from freshwater, then, is crucial. If they hit saltwater too soon, they will die.

For that and other reasons, the salmon enter the most perilous period of their lives when they move into the estuary of the Fraser River. Most will not survive.

CHAPTER THREE

INTO

THE BLACK BOX

From a small plane high above the Strait of Georgia you can see how the flow of the great river spills far out into the sea. The waters of the Fraser River are clouded with glacial sediment carried to the coast from the Rocky Mountains. Roiling ocean currents dilute and tear at the freshwater of what is known as the Fraser Plume, slowly turning it a milky green. Eventually it all merges into blueness as it fades off to the horizon.

To the south of the river mouth lie Boundary and Mud bays, where the rich flats no longer support shellfish harvesting because of pollution; to the north are the beaches of Vancouver, which are often closed to swimming each summer due to high fecal-coliform counts. In between lie the undulating marshlands of the Fraser estuary — which have been reduced by 70 percent in the last century because of industrial and commercial developments. The tidal flats are among the most important salmon nurseries in the world, but decades of pollution have left them laced with chlorophenols, polycyclic aromatic hydrocarbons and dioxins. It's not hard to figure out why. There are about 40 wood-processing mills on the Lower Fraser, and the river collects sewage discharge from more than 30 communities. The Greater Vancouver area alone pumps out 1 billion litres of sewage a day. Added to that is the untreated runoff from more than 100 storm drain outlets, discharges by chemical plants, marinas sheltering 4,500 boats, log booms, ditches

OPPOSITE PAGE: Looking down the Fraser to the Strait of Georgia. The Fraser River estuary lies in B.C.'s Lower Mainland, home to over 2 million people.

that drain old garbage dumps, and runoff from croplands and golf courses treated with pesticides and fertilizers.

In the 1970s, scientists identified the collective environmental stresses in the Fraser as a serious problem, and government responded by targeting it for a major cleanup. But the project soon unwound. No serious effort was made to enforce pollution laws, and scientific research funding was virtually nonexistent. As the environmentally aware 1990s dawned, however, both provincial and federal governments showed a renewed commitment to the river, launching some major studies under a new Fraser Basin Management Program and promising, this time, to follow through. We shall see. Certainly the Fraser is worth protecting. Even producing at half its historical level it is the greatest salmon river on the planet. And its potential is amazing. The run of more than 22 million salmon that came back in 1993 could be doubled — and that figure could possibly be doubled again. For the river to produce to its fullest potential, however, the estuary must be

As they move into the estuary, salmon enter a two-layered world, where freshwater flows seaward along the surface and saline water flows landward at a lower level. The mix produces a rich, high-energy environment that nurtures salmon during a crucial period of life — but it is also a highly stressful and dangerous time.

kept healthy, and that is a difficult challenge.

The estuary remains in relatively good shape today because of the massive dilution that takes place. The river has a flow of 2,700 cubic meters per second. But even that is not enough to cleanse it of all the effluent, which settles out in quiet water, seeping into the estuary marshes and entering the food web. The sterile eggs of Great Blue herons that feed along the river, and the tumors that have been found in bottom fish in Vancouver harbor, testify to the seriousness of the threat.

Millions, perhaps billions, of young salmon rely on the Fraser as a nursery area as they make their dramatic and dangerous transition from freshwater to saltwater. They move through the tidal marshlands in pulses, feeding on small aquatic creatures and using the cover of weeds to escape predators. Traces of pollutants collect in the fish, but nobody seems to know yet exactly how serious that is. Does it

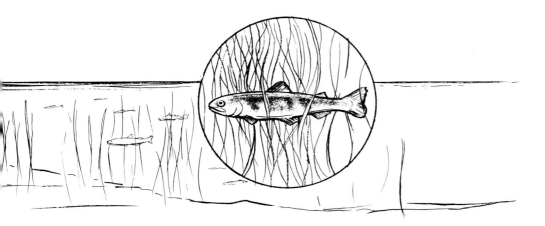

weaken the smolts in some way, making them more susceptible to disease or pre-dation? Or are the levels so minute that they are of no real consequence? Because of new provincial environment laws, the average daily discharge of dioxins by mills on the Fraser has dropped by 98 percent since 1990; furan levels have declined by 85 percent. That is a significant improvement and it demonstrates what the government can do when it has strong regulations. But a spectrum of pollutants — resin and fatty acids, chlorinated phenols and other substances which have an unknown effect on salmon — continues to flow into the river.

It is perhaps an undeserved blessing for society that the outmigrants from the Adams River sockeye run make only limited use of this troubled estuary. Unlike some species, which tarry for a year in the marshes, the glistening silver sockeye move fairly rapidly out into the Strait, carried by the Fraser Plume.

Foreshore development
characterizes much of
the lower Fraser River.

And again, as we see so often in the life cycle of sockeye, there is an amazing synchronicity with the environment. Just as the smolts make their debut in the sea, in March and April, the plankton biomass in the surface waters of the Strait of Georgia is blossoming, providing rich grazing areas for the young salmon.

In late April, sockeye smolts from the Adams are concentrated just off the mouth of the Fraser in the Fraser Plume itself, an area that has a wealth of food resources and a low salinity level. By late May the smolts are along the east and west sides of the outer Gulf Islands, feeding in the rich shallows along the shores of Mayne, Saturna, Saltspring and Galiano islands. By June they are concentrated in the islands, particularly along the east shore of Vancouver Island.

Most sockeye leave the Strait in late June and July. Some move south and then west, following the initial direction of the Fraser's flow and taking the major shipping route out through Juan de Fuca Strait. But the majority turn north, going up the Strait of Georgia, perhaps because they are pushed by powerful reversing tides that move faster than they can swim.

From April to June, sockeye smolts caught in the strait are about 8 to 12 centimeters in length, little changed from the size they were in the river. Those caught by researchers in the Gulf Islands averaged 1.5 centimeters longer than those taken in the Fraser Plume, suggesting that the bigger fish move farther, faster.

Some young-of-the-year sockeye migrate out of the Fraser at the same time as the one-year-old smolts. These younger fish, which are still fry, appear to rear in the estuary for several weeks, and of course are much smaller, averaging about 3.9 centimeters compared to the 9.5-centimeter smolts. Sockeye smolts in the Strait feed on insects, tiny shrimp-like animals called euphausiids, crab larvae and small fish.

Fisheries researcher M.C. Healey, who studied the movements of the young salmon, believes that pink, chum and sockeye smolts all concentrate in the Gulf Islands during the spring, quickly creating a food shortage. By June the salmon are forced to move on, like a herd of cattle that has over-grazed a pasture.

Scientists know there is a tremendous mortality rate during these early weeks and months in the sea, but they aren't yet sure of the causes.

"We understand less about the first few months that Pacific salmon spend in the ocean than all other phases of their life history. Mortality during these first few months at sea may be heavy and possibly critical to the numbers of returning adults," says Healey.

Just as the smolts make their debut in the sea, the plankton is blossoming, providing rich grazing areas for the young salmon.

Studies have indicated that while early ocean mortality is high, rates decline as fish grow larger. A study of chum salmon in the Hood Canal found 31 to 46 percent were killed per day for the first four days in marine waters. And it has been said that more pink salmon die in the first 40 days in the ocean than in the remaining 410 days of their lives. In a study of sockeye, it was estimated 90 percent of the ocean mortality occurs during the first four months.

"Unfortunately, the possible causes of mortality — predation, starvation, advective losses, osmotic stress, disease — are poorly understood," says Healey. "Predation seems the most likely cause for most of the marine mortality of salmonids. The conventional wisdom is that the inverse relationship between size and mortality is a function of outgrowing or outswimming predators."

A study of Fraser River pink salmon established a correlation between temperature, salinity and survival. When the sea was colder and more saline, more fish survived. Some scientists believe that's because Pacific hake and Pacific mackerel

*There are still quiet
spots in the estuary.*

invade nearshore areas during years when temperatures are higher — preying on juvenile salmon.

In his book, *Ocean Ecology of North Pacific Salmonids*, William G. Pearcy laments the lack of knowledge about the life of salmon at sea. "In a sense, the marine ecosystem has been neglected as an unfathomable 'black box', into which young salmonids disappear and from which, if all goes right, adults emerge," he wrote after studying marine fishes for more than four decades.

Still, a lot has been learned about salmon in the past 50 years. Not long ago it was assumed the fish went a short distance beyond the river mouth and milled around for a few years before returning to spawn. Many biologists believed that if the salmon ventured to sea, they'd surely get lost.

Now, after extensive tagging research, the outward and inward bound migration routes of salmon have been mapped, and it's known they travel thousands of kilometers across the Pacific, at times moving in direct lines at an incredible pace — as if they knew exactly where they were going and when they had to be there.

After cropping off the plankton bloom in the southern straits, the sockeye smolts begin to move north, through the Strait of Georgia, heading for Queen Charlotte Strait and the Inside Passage to Alaska.

Initially the herring-sized fish are easily pushed about by surface currents and river plumes, but they progress steadily north, and as they grow they become better swimmers. The fish are now a luminescent blue color on their backs, and a silvery white below. It is perfect camouflage. From above they are the color of the sea; from below they are the color of the sky.

Moving north along the coast, sockeye are helped by the Alaska Current, which generally flows counterclockwise through the Gulf of Alaska. Wind and freshwater inflows create many eddies and meanders, but the small fish make remarkable headway. It has been estimated that juvenile Fraser sockeye travel 1,000 to 2,900 kilo-

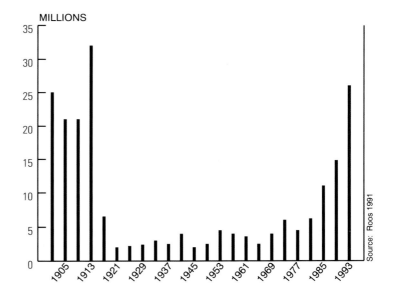

MILLIONS

Source: Roos 1991

meters in 66 to 123 days after leaving the river. One scientist calculated their speed of travel at two body lengths per second, meaning the fish were swimming north up to seventeen hours per day.

Going up along the coast of British Columbia the small salmon begin to ride the Alaska Current into the Gulf of Alaska. As it moves north the current narrows and intensifies into a deeper, westward flowing current known as the Alaska Stream. Slowly the fish are swept towards the Aleutians.

As the Adams River sockeye move north they are joined in the ocean by young salmon pouring out of hundreds of rivers and streams along the coast. Some of the rivers are unloading pink fry, others turn out chinook, coho, chum or sockeye. The fish are generally moving in the same direction during the same season,

The Hell's Gate slide in 1913 wiped out the Upper Adams run. The sockeye have come back in that cycle — but not to the Adams. These sockeye are headed for the Horsefly River.

spring, so there obviously must be areas where they cross paths. The stocks don't travel together, however. The vastness of the ocean environment, preferences for different temperatures, and other factors keep them separate. It may be the same as different flocks of ducks migrating north, travelling in small groups but homing in on a general nesting area.

During this period the sockeye stay relatively close to shore, feeding in the rich waters of the continental shelf zone, the most productive area in the Gulf of Alaska. Plankton crops here are several times greater than those found in oceanic waters offshore.

As the fish grow they seek out larger prey. Squid have been found to be the most important prey in central subarctic waters for coho, steelhead, pink and sockeye. When squid are available, the salmon gorge on them. But, unlike other species of salmon, sockeye also feed heavily on plankton and tiny water organisms. Some studies have indicated sockeye seek out areas with heavy crops of large zooplankton, perhaps finding the feeding areas with their temperature-sensitive bodies.

As the first year at sea ends, the sockeye are spread over a vast area, rotating slowly down into the North Pacific from below the Aleutian Islands, then swinging north again for another year of feeding. They will put on about 95 percent of their body weight during their two years at sea.

The factors that govern the survival of salmon at sea are not well understood, but there are clear links to El Niño, ocean upwellings and changes in atmospheric pressure.

Episodic El Niño events, in which warm water currents flow into the North Pacific from the Southern Hemisphere, are known to coincide with poor fishing years on the West Coast.

One effect the warm water has is to flood the area with new predators, such as mackerel, which feed heavily on young salmon. Areas such as Barkley Sound,

Little River looking east towards Shuswap Lake.

Digging a redd.

After the spawn.

Viewing the sockeye along the Adams River.

Above Shuswap Lake looking west.
Little Shuswap Lake is in the distance
to the left; Adams River is on the right.

A quiet backwater along the Adams.

Bunchberry along the
banks of the Adams.

Rainbow trout.

Western painted turtle.

*Early morning on
Shuswap Lake.*

which gets millions of sockeye smolts from Great Central Lake, are usually swamped with mackerel during El Niño years.

Another less obvious, but perhaps more damaging El Niño effect is the damper it puts on deep ocean up-wellings, which bring ni-trate-rich nutrients to the surface. When the up-wellings subside, as they do in El Niño years, plankton stocks crash. The density of zooplank-ton over the continental shelf, where young sock-eye congregate, is reduced by 70 percent in El Niño years. In 1982-83 the im-pact of El Niño was re-flected in a study in Oregon, which found fewer salmon returned to spawn that year, and those that did were smaller than usual.

This diagram shows the range and general migration pattern of sockeye stocks.

In 1994, Canadian fisheries scientists Richard Beamish and Daniel Bouillon reported finding a strong correlation between catch statistics and changes in atmos-pheric pressure over the North Pacific. As the pressure of the atmosphere increases or decreases, so too do the upwellings in the ocean.

Beamish and Bouillon studied the behavior of the Aleutian Low Pressure System — a large-scale climate system that dominates the North Pacific, sitting over the area favored by pinks, chum and sockeye — over several decades. They found changes in the system reflected in salmon catches by Canada, the United States, Japan and Russia — the four countries that primarily fish the North Pacific. "The strong similarity of the pattern of the all-nation pink, chum and sockeye salmon catches suggests that common events over a vast area affect the production of salmon in the North Pacific Ocean," they concluded.

During this century the commercial fishing fleet had high catches in the 1930s, falling off through the mid-60s then rebounding. The researchers found catches dropped when the Aleutian Low declined. Catches rose when it increased.

There are many other climatic variables at work in the North Pacific, of course. And there are human factors too. The Japanese began hatchery production of salmon in 1887 and by 1892 were releasing 16 million fish, possibly affecting wild fish production. In Canada there was a decline in catch in the early 1900s related to overfishing and, after 1913, due to rockslides in the Fraser canyon. Nonetheless, the research by Beamish and Bouillon appears to have made a strong link between the Aleutian Low and ocean productivity.

If so, catches will rise and fall in a natural rhythm that is uncontrollable by humans. That has significant management implications, because when catches decline, commercial and sports fishers demand action from the Department of Fisheries. The most rapid way to respond to that pressure is to start pumping more salmon out of hatcheries. But Beamish and Bouillon warn it may not be smart to release large numbers of artificially reared smolts when nature is dictating lower survival at sea.

If nothing else, the research by the two scientists highlights how complex the world of salmon is, and how little is known about what's going on in the black box. One of the biggest mysteries is how the salmon find their way home again.

Every summer in July, millions of sockeye suddenly come flooding back into Bristol Bay, Alaska. The fish are returning from feeding areas far out in the Pacific. They are coming in from widely dispersed points, with some returning from the Aleutian Islands and others from the open ocean far to the south. An amazing thing happened when researchers tagged and released salmon at scattered points in the North Pacific. They found the fish arrived back at the same time, despite travelling by different compass headings, on routes of varying length. And a review of fishing data collected over a 30-year period showed the run changed little in its timing over the decades; it always returned within the same twelve-day period in July. Individual stocks on average only deviated by two days. To arrive so closely packed, the fish either had to migrate at different speeds, or those coming from farther afield had to start earlier.

The Bristol Bay sockeye, as do the Adams sockeye, swim near the surface, so they don't follow underwater valley and mountain formations, the way migrating birds do on land. They criss-cross major currents, so they do not swim upstream to get to open ocean and downstream to get home. They might rely on celestial navigation, but the weather is often stormy and overcast, so they can't always see the stars.

There are many theories about how salmon know where to go, and when to leave in order to arrive at a set time. Some of the factors at work, but not completely understood, are their sensitivity to polarized light, the way they measure the length of the days by sending signals about sunlight to a special gland in the head, the detection of pheromones or other chemicals in the water by their olfactory cells, and their ability to detect electrical currents and magnetic fields.

Researcher Robert Burgner argues that the most likely explanation lies in a salmon's genetic makeup; that the patterns of migration are stamped on its brain.

"During the great distances salmon travel in the ocean, they clearly rely on inherited responses to guidance stimuli. These fish have had no opportunity to learn from parents. They migrate over broad expanses of the ocean and often travel circular routes not traversed in reverse on the return journey," he says.

"It is clear, however, that strong migration patterns are genetically determined. Salmon progeny transplanted to radically new environs, such as Okhotsk Sea pinks to the Barents Sea, stray extensively from their new 'home' stream. Apparently they experience great difficulty in finding a route back in a foreign ocean environment."

Experiments on the sensory cues used by salmon in the ocean haven't been conducted yet, so scientists are still largely guessing about what takes place. But there

WILD vs. HATCHERY SALMON

It is thought there is little mixing of wild and hatchery salmon in the ocean, because the timing of release and offshore migration is not matched. Some researchers have noted, however, that when large numbers of hatchery fish were released during periods of weak ocean upwelling, there was a decline in the abundance of both hatchery and wild fish, giving rise to a theory that the ocean can only support so many fish at any given time.

has been substantial experimentation on salmon in freshwater and there is no reason to believe the sensory mechanisms used by outmigrating salmon would not also be used by those coming home.

Sockeye salmon smolts in tanks orient themselves in appropriate compass direction using the sun or polarized light. Pink salmon show a similar trait, displaying their strongest orientation when the sun is visible above the testing tanks. Some salmon are able to maintain their directional sense even when the tank is covered, leading researchers to conclude the fish can detect the earth's magnetic field and don't need any visual clues.

The whole question of how salmon know what compass heading to take, no matter where they are, is 'the major puzzle' facing fisheries scientists today.

"Uniformly magnetized crystals found in the cranial tissue of sockeye and chinook salmon are probably used for detection of the direction of magnetic fields. Therefore, we may assume that the earth's magnetic field can be used to maintain a course in the ocean," William Pearcy says.

Other researchers have speculated on the ability of salmon to orient themselves using the electrical currents that are created when a conductor such as sea water moves through the earth's magnetic field. Atlantic salmon have demonstrated this ability, but it isn't known if Pacific salmon have the same talent.

Olfactory senses do not seem to play a part in ocean migration. In one experiment, salmon had their olfactory nerves severed; they still knew which direction to go, at least until they hit the estuary.

The pineal gland, located in the forebrain, seems to be a triggering mechanism for telling salmon when to start their epic migrations. The gland, known as a "third eye," receives light signals from the eyes. When the days get longer in the spring, the pineal gland stimulates hormonal activity. Even in blind fish, however, the pineal becomes active, prompting a display of spawning colors. How the third eye gets light when the real eyes aren't working isn't known.

And Pearcy says the whole question of how salmon know what compass heading to take, no matter where they are, is "the major puzzle" facing fisheries scientists today.

"We must be open to the fact that the sensory world of salmonids is far different from ours, and unexpected capabilities may be discovered in the future," he says.

In other words, there are forces at work that, at the moment, are beyond our imagining.

Whether it is the length of the days, the glimmering of the stars at night, or changes in the earth's magnetic field, there is no mistaking the migration signal when it comes. When the trigger is pulled, the mature salmon turn east and begin to swim directly towards the coast. Some of them are coming back from journeys that have taken them out past the tip of the Aleutian Islands to near the coast of southeastern Siberia. Some are returning from the Bering Sea, north of the Aleutian chain.

Fraser River sockeye that were tagged 1,000 kilometers or more from the river were found to have traveled at more than 45 kilometers per day when they headed for home. The optimal swimming speed of a sockeye is about 43 kilometers per day — which means the fish must swim along a nearly direct course, day and night.

Fraser sockeye vary in the route they follow. From 1957 to 1977 most came on a southern track, moving down the outer coastline of Vancouver Island and hooking up through Juan de Fuca Strait, into the Fraser Plume. From 1978 to 1985, however, most returned by a northern route, turning inside at the top of Vancouver Island and coming down through Johnstone Strait. That was their route of choice in 1993, which led to phenomenal commercial salmon catches in the narrow passes north of Campbell River.

The route seems to be selected by sea-surface temperatures along the west coast of Vancouver Island and the Queen Charlotte Islands. In warm (El Niño) years the fish appear to be farther north in the Pacific when they head for the coast, which results in a landfall north of Vancouver Island. In cold-water years the fish are to the south, and loop up around the southern tip of Vancouver Island.

Whichever route they take, the salmon become the major focus of the British Columbia commercial fishing fleet once they have reached nearshore waters. Every fisherman, every fishing community, knows when a dominant Adams River run is coming back. For many, dreaming of it, hoping for it, has been all that has kept them going through the lean years. The big Adams years have always been a time to cash in — but far more important than that, the strong runs have reminded everyone of what the fishing could be, fuelling hope for better years in the future.

Originally, chinook were the main fish the fleet sought. But due to overfishing

Ranging far across the open Pacific, sockeye feed heavily on phytoplankton, free-floating microscopic plants and on larger prey like squid, lantern fish and juvenile cod. Seals, sea lions, killer whales — and humans — in turn prey on the salmon.

and habitat damage, chinook stocks declined, and commercial boats turned more and more to sockeye. Sockeye are famed for their rich meat and the fine flavor the fish holds, even in the can. It was the red meat of canned sockeye that, more than anything else, helped British Columbia salmon gain a global market. So it came as a devastating blow to the industry when sockeye stocks declined after the 1913 slides in Hell's Gate. Up until then, sockeye had accounted for 60 percent of the catch. After that, the sockeye catch fell to only about 16 percent of what it had been. Chum and pink salmon became the mainstays of the commercial fishery. But with a resurgence of sockeye stocks in the Adams, Horsefly and Skeena rivers, commercial boats have increasingly returned to catching the red salmon. Gillnetting, in which a wall of net is laid out behind a boat, entangling fish, and seining, in which a net is set in a circle and pulled into a purse-like trap, are the two main

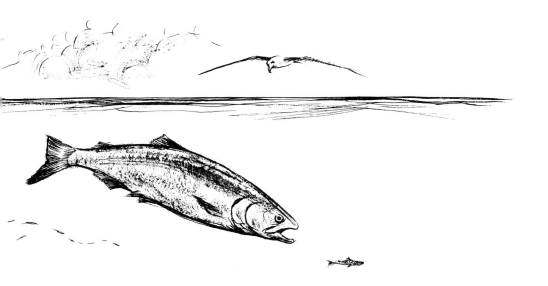

With the opening horn sounding, seiners rush to make their first set.

ways of taking sockeye. The relatively narrow inlets leading up to the Fraser and the Skeena River on British Columbia's north coast, are the fishing areas of greatest importance.

The proficient manner in which the commercial fleet sweeps the ocean with nets has led to some major environmental concerns in recent years. While sockeye have been returning in the tens of millions, other species of salmon have not been faring so well. Chinook, coho and steelhead — the rarest of the salmon species — have all been hit hard by the commercial fleet.

Because the salmon species largely follow the same routes once they are inshore, and because nets can't discriminate between them, small stocks can be wiped out if they run into a gauntlet of nets set for a larger run of fish.

Steelhead stocks in the Skeena and Thompson Rivers have been particularly damaged by sockeye and chum fisheries, raising concerns about the endangerment of these tremendously important stocks. Efforts are being made to resolve the problem. Among other things, the commercial fishing industry has been working to develop new methods of netting that would be more stock specific. By setting their nets deeper, for example, fewer steelhead will be caught because they run closer to the surface than other species. Many commercial operators oppose the deeper nets, however, because sockeye also often swim close to the surface and can escape. One argument put forward by the commercial fishing industry is that runs of steelhead should simply be made larger. But that is not easy to do. Hatcheries might be able to achieve that goal, but the cost would be the loss of genetic stock that took tens of thousands of years for nature to develop.

The Steelhead Society of British Columbia, an organization that represents sports fishing interests, has said gillnets should be banned on environmental grounds and commercial fishers should be made to take their catch from fish traps set in the rivers. By using traps, which funnel fish into a fenced pool, the harvest can be carefully controlled. The exact size, number and species of fish to be caught could be selected from the holding pool and the rest of the fish could be set free. It sounds like a revolutionary idea — but the Indians thought of it first, and had traps in use when the first Europeans arrived. The weirs were later ordered removed by the government, which argued that the method endangered salmon stocks. A shift back to traps would cause tremendous upheaval in British Columbia's existing commercial fishery, which is a vital part of the social and economic fabric of the province.

One solution to the problem lies in the radio tagging work that has provided biologists with precise data on the timing of endangered steelhead runs. It's now possible to shepherd a run of fish through the commercial fleet by closing the fishery at certain times and places along the migration route. The fishing industry opposes such closures because millions of sockeye can slip through when an area is closed to protect only a few thousand steelhead. But clearly something has to give, or relatively small but valuable stocks of wild chinook, coho and steelhead could be wiped out during the mass harvest of sockeye or chum. Once gone, the genetic coding locked in those unique stocks would be lost forever.

It has taken decades to figure out the timing and location of the many different runs of salmon that return to the rivers of British Columbia. The first pieces of the puzzle began to fall into place in 1918, when a tagging experiment with sockeye was conducted in Juan de Fuca Strait. That year, 831 sockeye were tagged off Sooke, on Vancouver Island. Of those fish, 147 were later recovered, establishing for the first time that the fish had a definite route up through Juan de Fuca Strait, north through Rosario Strait, past Point Roberts and on to the Fraser River.

In 1925, a tagging of 519 salmon established another route from Deep Water Bay, at the southern end of Johnstone Strait, to the Fraser.

Japanese and Alaskan biologists were also tagging sockeye during the 1920s, and the deep ocean pathway of the salmon was slowly beginning to take shape.

Until the tagging experiments of the 1920s, many scientists had believed that if salmon did in fact return to the stream of their origin it was only because they never went far from the estuary once they reached the sea.

The tracking showed that salmon from the Fraser were crossing the straits — and returning. Some scientists found it hard to believe. As late as 1925, fisheries authority David Starr Jordan was dismissing the proposition that each river had a distinct race that came home to spawn. "It is the prevailing impression that the salmon have some special instinct which leads them to return to spawn on the same spawning grounds where they were originally hatched. We fail to find any evidence of this in the case of the Pacific salmon and we do not believe it to be true," he boldly stated, despite growing evidence to the contrary.

Other scientists, however, were convinced salmon did return to their home stream. Charles H. Gilbert, who studied sockeye in the Fraser, had concluded as early as 1918 that a very complex and refined system was at work. He suspected that not only did each river have its own distinct stock, but that there were separate runs within rivers.

"To one who watches pass before his eyes this process of types possessing a certain uniformity, who detects, as it is so often possible, the advance skirmishes of the next invasion when they make their first appearance during a transition period, who watches the new type becoming the dominant one and the old form soon represented by only a few stragglers — to such an observer the connection seems inescapable that the run consists of a number of sub-races, each bound to its own spawning area within the Fraser basin . . . If this theory be true, not only do sockeye salmon return to their own river-basin at maturity, they predominantly return to the particular part of the river-basin in which they were reared as fingerlings, in which case their homing instinct is far more rigid in its workings than heretofore has been accepted."

As the tagging data built up, it became clear that Gilbert's intuition was right. Each river did have its own stock — and each stock was uniquely programmed.

CHAPTER FOUR

IN THE MIND OF
THE FISH

The Adams River sockeye hesitate when
they hit the Fraser Plume on their return journey. The first fish arrive as early as
August and the run continues to build until mid-September. Starting in the spring,
with early chinook, runs of coho, pink, chum and sockeye have been locking on
to the freshwater signature of the big river and turning in out of the Strait of
Georgia. Some of the runs bolt straight into the mouth and vanish. But the Adams
stock does not. Sometimes for weeks the fish feed heavily just outside the estuary
in an area known as the Sand Heads. This characteristic has made the Adams run
important to a small but rapidly growing cult of sports anglers.

Some sockeye are notoriously reluctant to take a trolled lure, but Tony Pletcher,
a Vancouver sports angler and retired college teacher, says the Adams run is different.

"The Adams fish are biters. Boy, are they biters," he says as he delivers a non-
stop monologue to a group of enthralled anglers at one of his fishing lectures.

Pletcher, who has raised sockeye fishing to the level of voodoo science, has been
catching Adams River sockeye off the mouth of the Fraser River for fifteen years.
He says that while commercial trollers long knew that sockeye would take a lure,
sports anglers until recently assumed the fish were uncatchable because of their
plankton diet.

With evangelical zeal, Pletcher has been spreading the word around Vancouver that not only do sockeye bite, but when the Adams run comes in, it puts the best fishing in the world right on the city's doorstep.

Pletcher favors a small plastic lure known as a hoochie. The lure, which looks like a tiny Hawaiian skirt, imitates squid, one of the sockeye's favorite prey items in the open Pacific. It

Sport fishers.

doesn't matter if there are no squid in the Fraser Plume. When the sockeye see that darting, red Hoochie, they want it. Pletcher trolls slowly into a tide change at first light, at precisely the right speed (one to two knots), with his Hoochie dancing at a depth of exactly 30 meters. He washes all his gear before he uses it, washes his hands, and rubs herring or salmon slime on his lures. When a dominant Adams run is in, he says, the fishing is incredible.

"Ten million fish," he cries to his audience. "Think of it!" The crowd of about 50 anglers is rapt and it's clear that when Pletcher next returns to the Sand Heads to orchestrate the dance of the voodoo Hoochie, he's not going to be alone.

Nobody's sure why the Adams stock gathers at the river mouth to feed so aggressively. But Scott Hinch has a theory. He thinks the Adams fish are loading up with energy for the dangerous and demanding journey that will take them up through Hell's Gate and into the boiling rapids of the Thompson River.

Hinch, a biologist with the University of British Columbia's Westwater Research Centre, headed a research team that in 1993 gained some profound insights into the life and death of sockeye in the Fraser River. He learned, among other

The Fraser is known for its powerful currents, whirlpools and eddies.

things, just how crucial energy loading is to migrating salmon.

Using new technology developed by Lotek Engineering of Ontario, Hinch wired sockeye with highly sophisticated radio transmitters. For years researchers have followed migrating fish by fitting them with tiny electronic devices that emit a radio signal, tracking them with handheld receivers. But Lotek's equipment allowed Hinch to do far more than just follow a beeping noise up the Fraser.

The signals he and his research team received came from electronic transmitters that were surgically implanted into the fish's muscles. The operation, which takes seven minutes, leaves a salmon with a thin antenna, like a guitar string, trailing from its belly. From the radio signals it is possible to tell not only where a fish is, but when it's resting or moving, how much energy it's using, and the temperature of the water it's swimming through.

As he followed salmon after salmon from Yale up to Hell's Gate (a 20- to 36-hour journey at speeds of 0.8 to 1.5 kilometers an hour), Hinch began to see the Fraser in a whole new way. He began to see it like a salmon.

"It was almost like being in the mind of the fish," he said of the countless hours he spent tethered to salmon by electronic signals.

As he trailed the sockeye he saw how they hugged the bottom in sections, slipping under the heavy main current of the river. He saw how they nosed into cracks and crevasses in the riverbank, hiding from the current like fry, and how they ducked into the mouths of small streams to get out of the Fraser's silt. During one spate he waited for the better part of a day while his tagged sockeye held in the clear water at the mouth of a small creek. The fish wouldn't move until the silt load in the Fraser had dropped. He saw how some fish swam day and night, and how others halted abruptly the moment the sun set. And he noted how some fish became disoriented in the powerful back eddies, sometimes swimming around and around for several hours.

Sections of the river that had seemed innocuous took on new significance when Hinch learned how the salmon labored to get up them. Certainly it was no surprise that salmon had trouble negotiating rapids in the canyon, but what he hadn't anticipated was the huge amount of energy needed to pass through apparently easy sections of the river. The biggest problem: relatively shallow, fast-moving water flowing through narrow channels created by gravel bars.

Hinch found that as the summer progressed and water levels dropped, salmon had an increasingly difficult time getting upriver. Eventually he recorded more than a dozen choke points where fish struggled to make headway.

"We noticed places where fish were delayed for many hours," he said. "The fish would try many times. You could see a fish move in and get blown back out dozens of times."

When a salmon enters the river it stops eating. The energy reserves it carries with it are all that it has. As each day passes, the salmon loses a percentage of its body weight as it burns up the fat it has stored for the journey. By the time it has reached its home river and completed spawning, its weight has dropped by two thirds. Some long-running stocks only have a few days of fat reserves, so any delay in the migration can be fatal.

Biologists know that each year a percentage of salmon die in the Fraser as they

A hoochie, a small plastic imitation of a squid, one of the sockeye's favorite ocean prey items, is used by sport fishers who troll for salmon.

A gillnetter taking its catch in the slow-moving waters of the estuary.

head upstream. Those are known as "inriver mortalities." Some, classified as "prespawning mortalities," die right on the gravel beds, just before mating. The causes of these sudden deaths of apparently prime fish aren't understood. Some years a significant number of fish die this way. It could be that they burn themselves out fighting to get home. Hinch's research shows the fish could easily exhaust themselves, particularly when the water is low.

"When you start adding up the hours salmon spend at these gravel bars you really start to knock away at that survival time," he says.

In some sections of the river there were hazards that remained a mystery because the wired salmon simply disappeared. The fish were swallowed up by the waters, and their $700 transmitters were never heard from again.

"They just vanished off the face of the earth," said Hinch, who thinks the fish must have died for unknown reasons and then sunk to such great depths the transmitter stopped working. Inriver mortalities.

In the Lower Fraser, salmon are taken by commercial fishing boats that operate on strictly controlled openings which might last several hours or a few days. As they move upstream, the salmon become the focus of a series of native fisheries. The natives, who fish with small gill nets strung from shore, can't match the commercial fleet for technology and massive catch capacity. But natives are extremely efficient fishers nonetheless. They set their nets in the small back eddies favored by salmon and make a steady catch. As effective as the nets of both native and non-natives are, however, some fish always manage to wriggle free. Some of those fish are later seen on the spawning grounds, with rope-like scars across their backs marking them as escapees.

In an effort to determine how much energy was used by fish struggling to get out of nets, Hinch put a number of salmon in gill nets in a tank and watched while they escaped. He found that if a fish had to struggle for more than a few minutes, there was a good chance it would later die before spawning, even if it did get free. And he noted that not all of the fish that escaped were marked by net burns. Fisheries managers have always counted scarred fish on the spawning beds in order to keep track of the number that encountered nets. It was assumed that unmarked fish had passed through the various fisheries unscathed. But Hinch's study shows even the unmarked fish may have been temporarily entangled in a net and subject to great stress.

He said that once a commercial fishery is set in motion on the river, "you can expect every fish in that section to get caught or encounter a net."

Once a commercial fishery is set in motion on the river, 'you can expect every fish in that section to get caught or encounter a net.'

What that means is that nets have a far greater impact than has been recognized. In an effort to keep track of the intensity of a fishery, managers have always relied on the dockside catch counts. That is, if 500 fishermen brought in 100 salmon each, it was assumed 50,000 salmon had been removed from the run. But Hinch's study suggests that for every fish counted at the dock, an unknown and perhaps significant percentage die either "inriver" or "prespawning." This raises serious questions about the management of stocks where eight fish are caught for every two that get to the spawning grounds. Could it be that salmon runs — even the prolific Adams stock — are being suppressed by fishing techniques that are far more wasteful than ever imagined?

In 1992, 482,000 sockeye that were estimated to be in the river during their homeward run failed to reach their spawning grounds. The disappearance of the fish, which were mostly early running Stuart River stock, came as a shock to federal fisheries managers. The department promptly closed the river to all fishing from August on that year. A subsequent investigation concluded that "unusually intensive fishing" in the Fraser was to blame.

Peter Pearse, a University of B.C. resources specialist, and Peter Larkin, a professor emeritus at UBC, said that a new native commercial fishery that opened on the river that year had been poorly managed, resulting in a massive loss of fish from the spawning beds. They believed that many of the fish had been taken by native fishermen, but never reported to authorities.

However, in a technical appendix to the formal report, Larkin said net-induced stress may have accounted for many of the missing salmon. He noted that 60 percent of the early Stuart fish on the spawning beds were net-marked. And he said native fishermen at Yale had commented on the number of dead fish seen floating downstream during the fishery.

Hinch found that the Hell's Gate fishway, built in 1944 and credited with saving Fraser River salmon stocks, doesn't work very well.

"Fish that had been caught and had escaped had undoubtedly been stressed by the experience and rendered much less capable of coping . . . While it is not possible to put a precise figure on these losses from additional stress and from drop outs, there is strong circumstantial evidence for a substantial mortality," said Larkin.

The researchers called for better management and increased surveillance and monitoring of the commercial catch in the river. Native fishing representatives challenged the accuracy of the government's spawning bed and inriver estimates, but agreed a better job had to be done in managing the fishery. In 1993 there was no massive disappearance of fish. Instead, there was a "surplus" of about 1 million, suggesting that spawning bed or inriver counting methods were suspect.

One disturbing find made by Hinch concerned the operation of the Hell's Gate fishway, which was built in 1944 and has been credited with saving Fraser River salmon stocks. Hinch found the massive concrete structure doesn't work very well.

"Hell's Gate was not built with fish behavior in mind,

Aerial view of Hell's Gate showing main fishways.

but hydrodynamics," says Hinch. In other words, it was built by engineers who thought like engineers, not like fish.

Rail line construction through the canyon in the mid-1900s left a jumble of rock piled at a narrow constriction in the canyon. Even after much of the debris was cleared, the water velocity was too high for most salmon to get past. The fishway was built as a massive concrete tunnel by-pass, in which a series of baffles slowed down the driving current of the Fraser, allowing the fish to reach quieter water above Hell's Gate.

Hinch does not question that the fishway works. But he says it may not work as well as has long been assumed. Half the fish he was tracking never made it through the fishway, getting blown out by the current, or making wrong turns at the entrance, only to be hurled back downstream.

"Very often they would get into the fish ladder and get confused by the water coming from all these different directions," he said. "The fish, once they got washed out, didn't usually make it back for a second try.

"I remember one fish that took two or three hours to get to the mouth of the fish gate. It made a wrong turn and got washed immediately down river two or three kilometers. He died overnight in the canyon."

O ne crucial issue that emerges from Hinch's work is the question of what happens when water levels drop in the Fraser. The fishway can pass 13,000 salmon an hour at optimum flows, but studies have shown that as water levels go down, the Hell's Gate fishway becomes increasingly difficult for fish to use. Hinch's radio tracking evidence makes it appear that the fishway is already marginal. Two factors threaten to make matters worse. One is global warming, which would increase water temperature to levels sockeye can't tolerate, but which seems to be out of the hands of fisheries managers. The other concerns the plans of a private corporation to reduce the flow of one of the Fraser's main tributaries, the Nechako River in northwestern B.C.

The Aluminum Company of Canada's (Alcan) Kemano II dam, which was approved by the federal government in 1987 but remained under review in the spring of 1994, threatens to reduce the flow of the Nechako by more than 80 percent.

Disturbingly, no consideration was given in the Kemano plan to the downstream effects of the dam, which could reduce water levels by 1.8 meters at Hell's Gate, possibly leading to fatal migration delays. Late-running stocks like the Adams fish would be particularly at risk. The Kemano II dam would also harm Nechako River stocks.

Hinch did not track salmon above Hell's Gate in the first year of his study, but in the future he hopes to follow sockeye all the way to their spawning beds, recording energy use at every stage of the journey. Some of the fish he tracks will be bound for the Nechako, where he will be able to see the impact of low water and high temperatures on fish that have already been weakened by their struggles in the Fraser.

When the federal government acted suddenly in 1992 to give native fishing groups on the Fraser the right to commercially sell their catch, the policy was attacked by many as unfair. The main criticism came from the commercial fishing industry, which has been in existence in British Columbia for about 100 years. Fishing boat operators were worried about their financial survival because the government was suddenly dealing a new player into the game. They argued that it was unjust for the government to award fishing privileges on the basis of race. But native leaders countered with a powerful argument — not only were the Indians here first, but they started the commercial fishing industry. Their right to sell fish had been stolen from them by the government a century earlier. So they weren't getting new rights in the summer of 1992, but old rights restored.

All the way from the mouth of the Fraser to the banks of the Adams River, sockeye run through Indian country. There are ancient village sites hidden on the terraces above the river, and there are drying racks being worked in fishing places that have been used for centuries.

Native people have fished the Fraser for 10,000 years.

Lytton, B.C., where the Thompson and Fraser rivers merge.

Drifting into the Fraser canyon one fall day, with walls of black striated rock rising all around us, we were looking at a river, at a fishing place, that had not changed much in thousands of years. Leaning out from the cliff walls, wherever a cleft in the rock created a back eddy, were long poles lashed to gill nets. These were the native fishing rocks, and the nets were set for sockeye.

We were drifting through Nlaka'-Pamux territory, above Hell's Gate. Upriver is the territory of the Secwepemc, which extends to the Shuswap lakes, and downstream, the land of the Sto:lo Nation. Both the Nlaka'Pamux and Secwepemc people are members of the Shuswap Nation. They all fish the Fraser for salmon, and always have. When Simon Fraser came through he found Indians fishing here, and used some of their canyon walkways to pass downstream. The earliest traders with the Hudson's Bay Company established a commercial dealing with natives for salmon. The first salmon exported from the province were caught by the Indians and sold to the Hudson's Bay Company at Fort Langley in 1829. Natives sold 7,544 salmon that year, and the next year sold 15,000, which were shipped overseas in barrels. In 1888 the government made it illegal for natives to sell the fish they caught. The intent, apparently, was to eliminate native competition in the growing fishery. But the natives never obeyed the law, continuing to operate a bootleg fishery that found a ready market. For more than 100 years, native fishermen traded on the black market. In recent years they had taken to running their fish around in the trunks of their cars like bootleg whisky, or brazenly moving freezer trucks of salmon out of the province. For this they were pursued in jet boats and helicopters, spied on by fisheries officers who stalked through the night woods in black-face, arrested by the hundreds and fined.

Historically, natives took all six species of salmon in the river, but chinook and sockeye were the most favored.

"Fighting their way up the canyon, hugging the banks to utilize every backwater and eddy, these fish were easily caught in dip-nets, and drew thousands of Indians to the banks of the river to reap the harvest," anthropologist Wilson Duff wrote in a 1952 report for the British Columbia Provincial Museum. "In earlier times, sockeyes were less favoured as food than springs and most were used for oil, but in more recent years, with the serious decline in the number of springs, an increasing number [of sockeye] have been caught for drying."

The warm, dry weather in the canyon, with a steady upriver breeze and the heat that emanates from the rocks at night, created perfect drying conditions.

Originally natives used dip nets in the canyon, but by the 1930s, gill nets set out from the bank with poles had become popular.

Ray Silver, an elder with the Sumas Band, grew up on the banks of the Fraser. His family used to live at the fishing grounds from spring through to late summer. He remembers the smoke house he played in and the wealth of old red, blue and white agate arrow heads he found on the beaches, where his people had camped for hundreds of years. Once he found an eagle carving, a medicine bowl used by a shaman.

"It's shallower all over now," Silver says of the river that is flowing beneath our inflatable raft. "Filled with silt down below. The Vedder [a tributary on the lower river] is changing because where it pours into the Fraser is filled with silt. It is

FISH SCALES

The scales of fish are like fingerprints, bearing clues that allow researchers to identify the lake in which the fish was reared. By scale analysis, scientists can determine the exact run to which a salmon belongs, and from its growth rings they can tell how old a fish is. The scales grow as the fish grows, creating widely spaced rings during the spring and summer when food is plentiful, and tight rings during winter when food is scarce.

terrible and getting worse. I never, ever dreamed I'd be buying drinking water, but I am now. When I was a kid I drank the Fraser."

Just above Hell's Gate we see a sockeye, already wearing its red spawning colors. It drifts along with us for a moment, apparently oblivious to the monstrous lime green raft just above its head. Its tail beats a slow rhythm, then it vanishes in the silt. Ahead we can hear the rapids. The boat is a strange looking affair: two long tubes connected by a floor that is open at the bow so water can run right through and out the stern. Darwin Baerg, owner of Fraser River Raft Expeditions, who is running the outboard, smiles as we drift towards the brink of Hell's Gate. The trip has been organized to give native elders and some guests a tour of their territory, as seen from the river. None of them have ever been through Hell's Gate before, so they are experiencing an old world through new eyes.

The river flows towards Hell's Gate with gentle porpoise leaps, its grey flanks stretching out, fluid and powerful. It sweeps down into a twisting maw of white water where you can see the current making 90 degree turns on itself.

The river flows towards the Gate with gentle porpoise leaps, its grey flanks stretching out, fluid and powerful. It sweeps down into a twisting maw of white water where you can see the current making 90 degree turns on itself. Just before we go in, Baerg starts chattering about the beautiful rock formations, and pointing out the radio tracking antennae that Hinch's research team has set up on the cliff high above us. We are through the white water almost before we have time to get scared. Almost. "That's probably 350 times for me through there," says Baerg. "It's different each time. You come through sometimes in high water and get inside those whirlpools, you know, the boat is 28 feet, and you're inside, looking up at walls of water."

Even below Hell's Gate the river is tumultuous, driving. Baerg looks at the river roaring past and says, "You know, it's hard to imagine salmon actually swimming through this."

He came through once when the Adams River run was here and saw the fish stacked up along the canyon walls, so deep you couldn't see the bottom of the school.

As we drift along, elder James Fraser looks up at the canyon walls and shakes his head. "You could be up there on the highway and never know this was down here. Isn't it pretty? Look how the sand has shaped the rocks."

We pass a fishing station. Two long-handled dip nets rest on the shore. "From time immemorial my people have used aluminum dip nets. It is a great tradition," Sonny McHalsie, a native anthropologist, says with a laugh. A moment later he points to a prominent bench of forested land above the river. "There are pithouses up there covered with 50- to 60-foot pines," he says. He points to another place where two native groups met for a battle. The land is resonant with history.

As we pass under the Trans-Canada Highway bridge just below the canyon, James Fraser is turning about, this way and that. Then he points. "That's where my place was. Had a house right there. That's my fishing spot. Not bad. Pretty good. Caught a big sturgeon there. Maybe fifteen feet long. This thick. Too big to haul him in. Butchered him right there in the river. Spread those big chunks around to everyone in the Nation. Even the [non-native] storekeeper got some."

He said that when he was a little boy there were lots of miners on the river, panning for gold and prospecting. "They lived in little cardboard houses, and we used to hear them singing on the river bars, their boxes rocking back and forth."

Along the river there are a series of big, gnarled rocks standing in the water. Native legend has it that when the Creator came through the country, following the river, he met a few of the local people. When he found some of them playing lahal, a gambling game, he got angry and turned them to stone.

"This one is bad," explains Fraser as we drift beneath the shadow of a huge boulder, caught in mid-gamble. "My mother told me whenever I came up the river I had to cross to the other side. This next one is broke. He lost everything."

We drift on, leaving the stone people behind. The elders point out berry-picking places, hunting places, and fishing place after fishing place. Beneath us, in the milky gray waters, the sockeye are passing upriver as they always have. They had sea blue backs when they first entered the river, but now they are turning red. The males are getting humped backs and big spawning teeth for intimidation displays and fighting.

They are going home, past the lahal players, past the rock giant known as Sucpin, or Cracked Head, out of the country of the Sto:lo, "The People of the River." Two days after passing Hell's Gate, the sockeye turn in to the clear waters of the Thompson River and go through the land of the Secwepemc, which means "Spilling out of the Waters," to where the river is born from Shuswap Lake. One of the last rock figures the sockeye pass is Skamamink, or "Big Belly," a pregnant woman who was turned to stone. Then, laden with eggs, they cross the lake and find the spawning beds of the Adams.

CHAPTER FIVE

MYTHOLOGY, SCIENCE AND THE NATIVE WAY

Th
here is a story native elders of the Shuswap tell about the destruction and resurrection of salmon. It is an old, old story that must go back to a prehistoric time when the salmon vanished — and then reappeared — as they have done before and as they may do again.

The story of the son of Tsotenuet links the importance of fish to humans and shows that the fear of losing our salmon is a recurring nightmare among societies of the Pacific Northwest. As well it should be.

When James Alexander Teit recorded the stories of the Shuswap Indians for the Jessup North Pacific Expedition in 1909, he thought they were all mythological tales. Perhaps they were, but like so many things from native mythology, the story of Tsotenuet appears to be interwoven with reality. The parable, in which a revengeful fish at one point takes human form, may be as true as anything ever written about salmon.

In the apocalyptical story, war is made on the fishes and all are killed save one, the pregnant wife of a large salmon-like figure called Tsotenuet. She soon gives birth to a son who is vilified by the people as a bastard and "little slave," for they have much to learn.

In native myths animals and humans often transform, changing shapes as easily as dancers slipping on masks. So it is not surprising that the son of the last living fish is described at times as a boy who joins human society.

The story takes a dramatic turn when Tsotenuet's son, whose name was never recorded by Teit, goes away to dream. Like a native on a vision quest, or a salmon returning from the sea, the boy goes to the mountains. And he gains thunder for a guardian. Thunder. Precursor of rain.

Cumulonimbus clouds form over the Columbia Mountains of the Shuswap with

dramatic suddenness, unleashing brief, intense downpours. In the spring, the rains flush nutrients into the lake, stimulating the growth of microscopic plankton and feeding the young sockeye. In the fall, the rains bring the spawning salmon in from the sea, not just by raising water levels, but also by sending scent signals to the olfactory glands of the fish. And atmospheric pressure plays a key role in determining how many salmon will survive their migration across the North Pacific. So there is a clear link between salmon

Pithouses, shelters sunk partially into the earth, were traditional winter homes for the Shuswap.

and the heavens, as the elders seemed to sense.

Coming down from the mountains, the fish-boy brings with him the power of lightning. That night the villagers dance, as they did in their houses along the salmon rivers in winter. The boy dances last and as he dances the house becomes hotter, until finally he shouts: "Come, strike!" Thunder strikes the house with lightning, setting it afire.

You have to imagine the scene now. All the people running outside and the boy too, dancing among the panic. Thunder towers over the village and wind rips at the trees. As the fish-boy dances he chants, calling on thunder again and again, and lightning flashes down, striking the people who had destroyed the salmon.

Soon all the houses are ablaze.

"Thus all the people and their whole village were burned and Tsotenuet's son had his revenge," wrote Teit. "While the fire was raging, his mother had hidden . . . Now she came forth, and they went to the fish country, where he jumped over the bones of his father and of the other people, and thus revived them."

Teit did not say where the story derived. Perhaps the Indians were in no mood to explain. But it seems to have stemmed from some cataclysmic event that took the salmon from the Shuswap people for a time. Scientists have recently unearthed evidence that, roughly 3,500 years ago, massive landslides blocked the Fraser near Hope. Today, from the Trans-Canada Highway east of Vancouver, near Agassiz, you can still see small humped mountains on the valley floor that are the remnants of the slides. The slides, perhaps triggered by a massive earthquake, shifted the river bed, and must have blocked the salmon for a number of years.

In the exposed walls of creek gorges along the banks of the South Thompson River, near the old Shuswap village sites, archaeologists have found white bands of volcanic ash, one layer of which coincides with the eruption of Mount St. Helens 3,200 years ago, and one marking the Mount Mazama eruption, which created Crater Lake 6,600 years ago. These "reliable geological time indicators," as geologists refer to them, are so distinct that an untrained eye can pick them out. When that volcanic ash first settled to the earth it must have been a fearsome event for the natives, with the dark volcanic clouds towering over the mountains like the God of Thunder. It may have devastated the salmon, perhaps filling in spawning beds with silt, and stifling the growth of plankton in the nursery lakes by cutting off the sunlight.

There were other events. Historical journals from the earliest traders in the Thompson River valley record years of hunger when the salmon failed to arrive. In 1829 they were starving at Fort Kamloops.

"This was because of a poor salmon run and the time spent trapping instead of hunting," the Secwepemc (Shuswap) Cultural Society reported. "Other years of starvation followed in 1841-43, 1850-52, 1855 and 1859."

In 1846 there was such a shortage of food at Fort Kamloops that the chief trader,

Hell's Gate in 1897. At this time salmon could probably swim through here without major difficulty.

John Tod, refused smallpox vaccination to 70 Shuswaps until they delivered a year's supply of salmon to his men. It isn't recorded if the Indians had the fish to spare, but Tod's apparently brutal tactic underscores the importance of salmon to both natives and non-natives alike. The salmon were the staff of life in the Shuswap, and the story of the powerful merchant trading medicine for fish seems almost biblical.

In 1857, another event shook the Shuswap — and again it was linked to a poor salmon run. That year a gold rush started up the Fraser and Thompson Rivers, and within twelve months over 30,000 miners, most of them from California, had flooded into the river valleys of British Columbia's south central Interior.

James Douglas, chief factor of the Hudson's Bay Company, wrote in 1857: "The native Indian tribes of Thompson's River . . . have already taken the high-handed, though probably not unwise course, of expelling all the parties of gold diggers . . . who had forced an entrance into their country . . . The Indians felt the gold was theirs as it originated from their lands. They also believed the activities of the miners would prevent the salmon from completing their migration up the Fraser and Thompson Rivers . . . The Indians . . . blamed the miners for the salmon run being small that year."

Lacking the power to call down lightning, the natives ultimately failed in their attempts to turn back the human tide that soon engulfed them. Miners camped on every gravel bar on the Thompson, took over fishing places, and washed silt into all the small streams that fed into the big river.

"The Indians complained that the miners interfered with their village sites, took their salmon, were disrespectful to their women and shot their children," wrote Douglas, giving some insight into the social turmoil that was taking place on the river.

The rush was short-lived. By the mid-1860s, gold was found up north in the Skeena, Cariboo and Omineca regions and the miners moved on. But by then many permanent settlers had arrived and the Shuswap, devastated by diseases brought by the new-comers, were no longer the dominant group.

One of the most serious blows to the salmon of the Shuswap came between 1911 and 1913, when railroad construction crews, blasting a bed through the Fraser River canyon, caused a series of slides. Fishing places are among the most valued posses-sions of native villages, and it must have been terrible for the people to see their sacred places blown into the river by dynamite. Worse still was the impact of a big slide at Hell's Gate in 1913, when debris choked the river. That year, early runs of salmon were wiped out when they arrived at the bottleneck

Fishing places are among the most valued possessions of native villages, and it must have been terrible for the people to see their sacred places blown into the river by dynamite.

during low water; the rapid was impassable. The Salmon River, which at the time had a sockeye run comparable in size to the Adams, lost its entire run of summer sockeye. The fish became extinct. (The Salmon River, which enters Shuswap Lake at the town of Salmon Arm, is now the focus of a community-based restoration effort, and small numbers of sockeye are repopulating the system.)

But despite the magnitude of the Hell's Gate blockage, the late-running Adams stock, which returns to the river between October 15 and 31, did manage to get through — because the water was higher in the fall than in the summer when earlier stocks were returning. There was thunder over the mountains and the rains came, raising water levels just enough to allow passage, and saving the salmon of Adams River.

Dipping for salmon along the Thompson.

In recording the Shuswap story of Tsotenuet, Teit uses a phrase that, because it is so eloquent and descriptive, must have been literally translated from the native dialect. To save the salmon, he says Tsotenuet's son and his mother returned "to the fish country." There may be no better way to describe British Columbia, where the mountains are laced with salmon rivers. The heart of that country must surely lie in the southern interior of the province, in the Shuswap, where tributaries of the Fraser River reach into an adjacent pair of ecodivisions known as the humid continental highlands and the semi-arid steppe highlands. It is there, where the Thompson and Okanagan Plateaus butt against the Shuswap Highland, near the southern extreme for sockeye salmon in North America, that Adams River is found — the most productive tributary of the Fraser, which in turn is the greatest salmon river on the planet.

On all maps and in all written references, the name of the river is given as Adams, but the 's' should really be possessive. The river is named after an old Indian chief, Sel-howt-ken, who was baptized as Adam by Oblate Father Nobli in 1849. His wife was named Eve. The couple, apparently the first natives in the area to accept the faith of the Most Holy and Immaculate Virgin Mary, lived on the shores of Adams Lake and had winter houses along the river. Given the fertility of the river and the nurturing role the watershed has played over the centuries, perhaps the river should have been named after Eve.

At any rate, Chief Adam died under the blessing of the cross when a smallpox epidemic swept through the Thompson Valley in 1862. The disease spread into the Interior along the trade routes, going up the Fraser and Thompson, following the path of the salmon. In the Shuswap the epidemic gained momentum in the fall, when the people gathered at Adams Lake to harvest sockeye.

One of the stories Teit heard when he travelled through the Thompson region was of Coyote, a powerful, magical figure who appears in native mythologies across North America.

Coyote was sent by "Old One" to travel the world and set right the things the creator had left undone. Among his miracles was the creation of the seasons and of day and night.

But Teit was told in the fish country that the greatest thing Coyote ever did was to put salmon in the rivers and make fishing places, which tells you something about the importance placed on salmon by native cultures.

The link between natives and the salmon is deep, and it stretches back a long time. The salmon came into the country first, probably 10,000 years ago as the glaciers retreated, and the Indians came not long after. They probably followed the salmon, as the fish pushed farther and farther into the mountains, seeking the source of the rivers. The native people in the Shuswap area speak Interior Salish, a variation of the same Salish language spoken on the coast.

During the Pleistocene epoch (1 million to 10,000 years ago) the Interior Plateau of the area that is now British Columbia was repeatedly glaciated. At least four major glaciations occurred in the northern hemisphere. It is believed the repeated appearance and disappearance of land and ice barriers created conditions that led to the development of different forms of salmonids.

When the glaciers retreated from the Shuswap, great stagnant chunks of ice standing in what is now Adams Lake were the last to melt.

At the height of the last glacial period, about 15,000 years ago, it is thought that there were no streams from the southern area of Alaska to the northern section of the State of Washington. The Yukon Valley, which was not glaciated, and the Columbia River to the south, may have provided the refuge rivers for salmon. After the glaciers melted, creating innumerable streams, the fish moved in, perhaps coming into the Shuswap from the Columbia drainage.

When the glaciers retreated from the Shuswap, great stagnant chunks of ice standing in what is now Adams Lake, and occupying the river valley, were the last to melt.

Scientists believe that because of the ice dam that once stood where Little Shuswap Lake now lies, the glacial river at first ran to the east and then turned south, going out through the Okanagan and eventually pouring into the great trench cut by the Columbia River. When the ice melted, the pattern of drainage reversed and the river swung to the west. If there were any salmon in the river at that time they would have been linked into the great Fraser River system, which opened access to much of British Columbia's Interior.

Among other things, the glaciers laid down a great fan of gravel that now forms

the perfect beaches on the Shuswap lakes and provides ideal spawning beds in Adams River. The glaciers also left dramatic silt benches along the South Thompson, which were well suited for Shuswap villages.

Usually settlements averaged eight or nine house sites, but at one site on the South Thompson, researchers counted 153 house depressions. They also found 21 mysterious rock structures — low, curving stone fences — up a steep gully on the north side of the river near Monte Creek. The petroforms, as they are called, may have been hunting blinds, food caches or kilns for preparing ochre. They may have been places for religious ceremonies. Perhaps it is where they went to pray

Looking east along the South Thompson to the town of Chase and Little Shuswap Lake.

for game — or the return of the salmon. Nobody knows.

Whenever archaeologists excavate village sites along the South Thompson they find salmon bones. And whenever the elders tell stories you can bet that, sooner or later, a salmon will swim through them in some prophetic or symbolic way. They ate salmon, they traded them, they built their mythology around them. Their culture was literally built on fish.

All along the Fraser and up through the Thompson to the Shuswap, native communities flourished along the rivers near productive fishing sites, where they caught salmon to dry for their own use and to trade.

A bear sculpture, from a burial site near Chase.

Between Kamloops and Chase a survey of the riverbanks found 192 archaeological sites. Many of the villages date back 4,000 to 5,000 years from the present, but it is clear natives were in the area long before that. The oldest known site is at Blind Bay on Shuswap Lake, where carbon dating showed material found in a cave was 9,000 years old.

During the summer of 1960, a burial site was discovered near the town of Chase, where you can look out across Little Shuswap Lake and see the valley of Adams River cutting through the mountains that have been rounded and shaped by glaciers. The site, which was thought to have been in use for a few hundred years, dates from A.D. 1750, placing it near the end of a period known as the Kamloops phase (A.D. 1250-1800), a time when villages prospered in the region. The end of that period coincides with the arrival of the first Europeans, when the Shuswap native culture went into a century of decline.

Sites like the one at Chase have yielded to archaeologists projectile points and other stone, antler, bone, shell, copper and wooden artifacts. In some sites fish spears and the remnants of nets were found, the tools of harvest. Burial and village sites have given up sea shells, traded in from the Coast, and arrowheads made of glassy basalt, chalcedony and chert.

In some graves researchers unearthed collections of small, smooth pebbles. They describe them as fetishes, objects believed to have some magical power. The stones are polished by the action of water, by the current of the river or the waves on the lakeshore. I understood why they were picked up and carried to the grave. Whenever I walk a river I look for stones like that. They must be slick and colored, and emanate a certain undefinable power. It seems if you find the right one the fishing will be good.

In another grave there was a green steatite bird bowl, small enough to fit in a cupped hand, with a hole drilled in the bird's head to hold a crown of feathers. When I saw it I thought of the shaman's eagle bowl elder Ray Silver found near his fishing place on the Fraser. The archaeologist recording the find describes the carving on the bowl as a bird of prey — but it is clear when you see it that it is an osprey. Ospreys live along the Shuswap lakes and you can sometimes see them diving out of the sky into the water to catch salmon.

"The carvings from Chase are important because they are the only steatite sculptures from a site known to be recent. Some relationship between these stone carvings and those [found at sites on] the Fraser delta is likely," David Sanger wrote in a report for the National Museums of Canada. He said that material found on the Fraser has been dated to the first millennium B.C.

Among the items uncovered near Chase were a pair of whalebone clubs, apparently of Nootka origin. The Nootka live on Vancouver Island, and how the clubs made that journey is not known, but the Shuswap were traders and they knew how to travel. They are known to have sent hunting parties east through the Rocky Mountains to get bison, for example, and salmon trails ran from the Shuswap into the Okanagan and Columbia River valleys.

At Chase, archaeologists found one of the largest collections of aboriginal artwork ever excavated from a single Interior Plateau site. The proliferation of art was linked to the salmon, which gave the people a bountiful food source and the free time they needed to be creative.

There are faces peering out from everywhere on the bone handles and other carvings — the faces of birds, bears, serpents and unidentified creatures. And from a

LOCAL PLANTS

Shuswap Indians made use of over 135 species of local plants. Big cottonwood trees, which grow along Adam's River, were used to build dugout canoes. Birch bark was used in basket making. The sinewy branches of red willows were used for fish weirs and constructing summer dwellings. Yew wood was used for making bows, and alder was a source of dye. Edible plants included service berry, soapberry, chokecherry, bullrush and cattails. Kinnikinnik was a form of native tobacco.

The Upper Shuswap Basin Fishing Authority maintains a fisheries management program throughout its territory. Here, a weir is built across a small creek and a fish count takes place.

child's grave this: toy arrows made from fish bones.

Sanger notes that because of the way some of the material was located on the graves, it seemed that the chipped knives, scrapers and digging sticks were suspended on poles above the graves. The material fell into the graves when the wood decayed. The graves, like the village sites, were usually located on benches overlooking the river, surrounded by bunchgrass and groves of chokecherry, hawthorn and alder. You can imagine what it must have been like to encounter graves at that time, with the knives rattling together in the wind and the sound of the river below.

Early photographs show the Shuswap were handsome people, with strong features and a proud look to them. But the material from archaeological digs indicates they were far more dramatic in appearance than even the best pictures reveal.

"Shuswap clothing was made from buckskin, mountain goat wool and rabbit fur. Feather head dresses were worn and large blankets were made from woven goat's wool," writes the Secwepemc Society.

Sanger's archaeological report adds these details about adornments: "The clothing was decorated with dentalium shells, wapiti teeth, glass beads and feathers. The body was frequently painted and occasionally tattooed. Pendants of copper, wapiti and deer teeth, beads of shell, seeds and bone and animal claws were suspended from the ears, nose, neck and hair."

There is no record of how Adam and Eve dressed as they wintered in underground houses on the banks of the river, living on smoked salmon stored in bark-lined pits. But we can guess. And it is clear that in their house of logs, poles, bark, moss and earth, as they danced and told stories, they were closer to the salmon than most of us could ever understand.

"The Shuswap people had their own spiritual beliefs. Life, for the Shuswap, included all living things," the Secwepemc Society says in its book, *Shuswap History: The First 100 Years of Contact.* "They believed that everything in nature had meaning and purpose. The people were connected, as one to the universe — through everyday life, through prayer, song and dance."

And they were connected, too, by their collective fear that the salmon would somehow be lost to them.

When the gold rush swept up from the Coast, the newcomers brought with them diseases which devastated the Indian villages. The Shuswap bands totalled 7,201 in 1850, but by 1903 the population had fallen to 2,185. The Adams Lake Band was 400, but fell to 189. The Little Shuswap Band went from 200 to 83. Smallpox, measles, diphtheria, tuberculosis, influenza and whooping cough were the big killers, and in those years it must have been even more devastating whenever the salmon runs were weak.

In the last 30 years, the Shuswap bands, like the sockeye salmon of the Fraser system, have been growing in number. The population now stands at about 6,500.

The Shuswap Nation Tribal Council — representing bands spread over 65,000 square miles bordered by the Columbia and Fraser rivers to the east and west, by the Bowron River to the north and by the city of Vernon to the south, and centred on the Adams River — has established a dynamic fisheries program. Native fisheries workers are involved in numerous habitat rehabilitation and salmon enhancement projects throughout the region. Their aim is to gain greater power in managing and protecting salmon stocks in their traditional territory. In a submission to the federal government's Standing Committee on Fisheries and Forestry in 1993, the Tribal Council pointed out that 57 percent of all the sockeye in the Fraser, 34 percent of the coho and 25 percent of the chinook spawn in Shuswap country.

"Shuswap peoples have endured a century of downstream activities that have adversely impacted their aboriginal right to access their fisheries resources," the Shuswap stated in their brief. "As early as 1910, in their Memorial to Sir Wilfrid Laurier, the Shuswaps cited declines of salmon and requested the Government of Canada to send their representatives to develop a treaty to protect their dwindling fishery resources. Today, the Shuswaps sponsor and endorse conservation efforts of clear benefit to all user groups that will return balanced salmon escapements to their territory and resurrect their traditional fisheries lost for the better part of the Twentieth Century."

By rebuilding spawning beds, operating hatcheries, collecting genetic samples of endangered runs and trying to get some say in the industrial developments that harm salmon, the Shuswap are taking new approaches to an old problem. Their way is less mythic than it once was. But they are doing the same thing Tsotenuet's son did when he went back to the fish country and jumped over the bones of his people. They are acting as guardians of the salmon.

CHAPTER SIX
THE DOMINANT
RUN

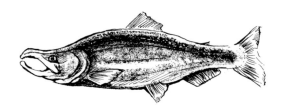

Whe railroad construction crews unleashed the disastrous Hell's Gate slide of 1913, salmon runs of the Fraser were already in decline because of overfishing. As canning methods improved, opening up a booming global market, commercial fishing pressure increased dramatically. In some years, 94 percent of the salmon were taken at the mouth of the Fraser. At the same time, population was growing in the Interior and salmon were being taken by an increasing number of settlers. The natural balance that the natives had had with the salmon was destroyed — and the result was tragic. Most runs were devastated; some vanished completely.

David Salmond Mitchell, the first fisheries officer in the Shuswap, saw the passing of the great runs early this century.

"These salmon runs were one of the Wonders of the World, and their loss has been one of the World's Greatest Disasters," he wrote in an unpublished manuscript in 1925. "These now lost salmon were everywhere described as 'inexhaustible.'

"Every stream was full of spawning fish. Little creeks or drains, too narrow for a salmon to turn in, and too shallow to cover the salmon's back, were used to the utmost."

One winter, at the end of a dominant run, Mitchell went to the Adams River to retrieve equipment from an egg-taking camp there and at nearby Scotch Creek. That year 15.5 million eggs had been collected from the two sites.

"After big runs the mouths of streams were hardly approachable for the stench," he reported. "For miles beyond the deep bars of dead salmon, the shores were strewn.

"On the 14th of December, 1905, we steamed through the awful stench into the wide bay at the mouth of the Lower Adams River. With mouths tightly closed we communicated only by signals. The shore was banked with a wide deep double bar of putrid salmon, extending around the bay until it faded out of view in the distance . . . We dropped a stern anchor, and crossing the slippery, putrid mound of rotting fish, in hip rubberboots, passed a bowline to a big cottonwood tree ashore."

The peak runs the Adams River now has are a reminder of those days when almost all the rivers of the Shuswap were overflowing with fish.

Mitchell wrote that human greed and ignorance were the main causes of decline.

"There was a natural balance, that was broken, when the white man came, and threw his rifle into it. He came, bang, bang, bang, at every living thing . . . The mink and otter were killed for their skins, and the eagles, ospreys, herons, loons, etc., perished as targets. As a consequence the coarse fish (ling, suckers, squawfish, etc.) eating the salmon eggs and fry, now increased enormously.

"With the development of canning at the coast the salmon runs were assailed at both ends.

"Then came settlers who ran amok when they saw the salmon run, killing them for pleasure after they had their barrels full, and slaughtering them for fertilizer.

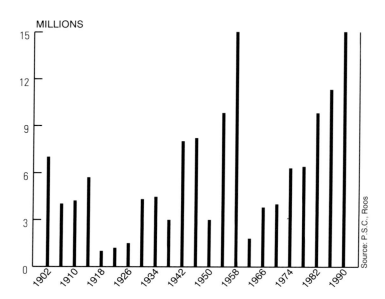

Source: P.S.C., Roos

The Adams River run announced itself in 1958 as the dominant sockeye run in B.C. It has in recent years increased to that level after the large decline in 1962.

Then came lumbermen's sluice dams.

"As the country settled up, the demand on the spawning beds became very heavy. It was an unsatisfied demand, as the canners allowed so few to pass, during three years out of four, that the settlers could only lay in a supply once in four years, when they used their chances to satiety."

W.E. Ricker, an eminent salmon researcher, has said the Fraser River may have had runs of 100 million sockeye during the early 1900s. And most of those salmon would have come from the Shuswap.

He says the runs were headed for disaster even before the Hell's Gate slide because they were being heavily overfished by the commercial fleet. Ricker says the Adams stock survived only because of fisheries closures that came into effect on the Lower Fraser late in the fall, coincidentally when the bulk of the run came through.

"There is one prevailing pattern among the salmon fisheries of the North Pacific Ocean," he writes. "Typically the rate of utilization of the stocks has increased to a point where annual recruitment and yield have declined, sometimes quite drastically. This phase is then followed by a period of rather painful retrenchment that has stopped the decline and, in some cases, has succeeded in increasing the yield again. In no case, however, has the mean annual production of natural stocks been restored to the level that prevailed for a few years at the peak of the expansion phase. Today's sustained yields are typically no more than 60 percent of the peak landings, and sometimes much less."

He says salmon runs were overfished because of "frontier exuberance and [the] absence of effective restraints . . . In fisheries it meant free-wheeling optimism and a fast-buck psychology on the part of some, but not all, of the operators. Much more important, probably, was the fact that recognizable indications of overfishing have always lagged several salmon generations behind the time when the optimum

'There was a natural balance that was broken when the white man came, and threw his rifle into it. He came, bang, bang, bang, at every living thing.'

rate of utilization was first exceeded. Thus overfishing could assume serious proportions before it was convincingly diagnosed."

As early as 1946 Ricker was warning about the need to let more salmon escape to the spawning grounds. He argued that reducing the catch would be ten times more beneficial than the impact of the Hell's Gate fishway, which was seen by many as the salvation of the Fraser. He was attacked for his views at the time, but fisheries managers later came to realize he was right.

The Adams River flourishes today because of a combination of circumstance, fisheries management, science, native faith and the miraculous resilience of salmon. It is not a freak of nature, but a reminder of how productive many of British Columbia's salmon rivers once were, and could be again.

In a distinct cycle of abundance that has never been fully understood, the Adams River turns red with a peak run of spawning sockeye every fourth year. There are spawners every year, but sometimes there are only a few thousand, and according to the federal government's Salmonid Escapement Database, on some years there are only a few hundred. In 1964, for example, only 716 sockeye were counted in the entire river.

But every fourth year the cycle hits a high point, known as the dominant run, and the fish return in the millions.

Since 1953 more than 19 million sockeye have spawned in this bright, perfect river. On an average year about 2 million adults run back towards the Fraser, and several thousand are allowed through the commercial fishery to spawn in the Adams. On a dominant year, 6 to 10 million fish return along the Pacific Coast, and about 2 million make it past the nets to the spawning grounds.

The dominant run coincides with 1994. That is to say that, because sockeye spawn on a four-year cycle, the big run of 1982 was repeated in 1986, 1990 and 1994. It is expected again in 1998, 2002 and so on. But it was not always so.

Moving back four years at a time you come eventually to 1922 — an epochal year in which Tsotenuet's son seemed called on to jump over the bones of his people again.

In 1907 the Adams River Lumber Company built a dam across the outlet of Adams Lake at the head of the Adams River. The year the dam was built, so many salmon gathered at its base, blocked from their spawning grounds in the Upper Adams River, that loggers boasted they could walk across the river on them. The image of salmon so numerous people could walk on them is a cliché for describing the once great abundance of salmon. But on the Adams, the year they closed the river, it was almost literally true.

The dam was used to store water that was released in floods to "flash-float" log booms down the river to Shuswap Lake. The booms went from there to Chase, where the American-owned company had established the largest sawmill in the Interior, the third largest in the province. The dam held Adams Lake at the level reached after spring melt, and log booms from the length of the watershed were stockpiled in the calm bay above the river. When the dam was opened, sudden walls of water swept downstream.

Sockeye schooling before pairing to mate.

Fisheries technicians making a beach set off the mouth of the Adams to collect sockeye for tagging.

The floods were so powerful they washed spawning salmon from the Adams River, and the jousting, hurtling flotillas of logs gouged the gravel beds, destroying nests. In between these terrible events the river was so low its bed was exposed, and incubating salmon eggs froze in winter or suffocated from lack of oxygen.

The operation, over a fifteen-year period, was so destructive that it seems fair to describe it as a war on the fishes. A huge run of sockeye that went up through the lake to spawn in the Upper Adams River became extinct because of the dam. The exact size of that run isn't known, but it was believed to be equal to the run in the lower river, ranging into the millions. For nearly 40 years the International Pacific Salmon Fisheries Commission has been working to restore the Upper Adams run, in some years planting up to 10 million eggs. The first signs of success came in 1984 — when a run of 3,000 fish came back. The river has the capacity to support several million spawners, but getting the runs back to historical levels has proved a nightmare because the unique genetic coding of the Upper Adams was destroyed when the stock became extinct.

In the Adams, the run barely stayed alive until the dam ceased operation in 1922. That was the year of rebirth. By 1954 the run had built to nearly 2 million spawners, a level that has been maintained, more or less, since then.

Before the logging dam was built the Adams run used to peak on a different cycle, in 1905, 1909, 1913 — and if it had continued, would have come in 1993, not 1994. It is possible that, had the logging dam and the railroad slide in the

Fraser canyon never happened, the Adams run could now peak in two years out of four, instead of one. But nobody knows for sure because the dominant cycle phenomenon has never really been figured out, although there are a lot of theories. Some feel it is a complex biological equation that is related to the impact each year's offspring have on the lake's plankton population. Others feel the cycle is not natural at all, but has been imposed on the river by human catch rates.

After the Adams River Lumber Company stripped all the old-growth forest from the Adams Lake region, processing 1 billion board feet at its mill, the company, owned by A.J. Lammers of Minnesota and J.P. McGoldrick of Washington, shut down the operation and moved away.

The dam was so destructive that it seems fair to describe it as a war on the fishes. A huge run of sockeye that went through the lake to spawn in the Upper Adams became extinct because of it.

"Although the company built the town of Chase and employed hundreds of men in the bush and in the mill, all of the profits went to business interests in the States. When the company pulled out in 1926, the area was left in a depressed state from which it took years to recover," the North Shuswap Historical Society reports in its periodical, *Shuswap Chronicles*. It also notes that at the time, loggers had been paid $2.75 a day, of which $1.25 was returned to the company for room and board. So the workers got a paltry amount for helping to destroy nature.

Looking back, it seems incomprehensible that a logging company would have been allowed to so devastate a salmon river. But it happened — in large part because, like the humans in Tsotenuet's story, people in those days had no reverence for the salmon. The fish spawned in such abundance in the late 1800s and early 1900s that few could have imagined the resource would ever be in jeopardy.

In 1913, for example, the Fraser River produced almost 2.5 million cases of canned sockeye. It is estimated 25 million salmon went into those cans, a large portion from Adams stock. Another 10 million were allowed to pass the gauntlet

A mature sockeye buck.

of nets, giving the Fraser an estimated run of 35 million sockeye that year.

But that was the summer of the great Hell's Gate slide, and only remnants of that massive run made it through to spawn. In the following years, the catches were so low the fishing industry almost went bankrupt in Canada and the U.S.

From that tragedy the International Pacific Salmon Fisheries Commission was born, in 1937, to protect, preserve and extend the sockeye fisheries of the Fraser. Its first big project, jointly funded by Canada and the U.S., was to build a $1 million fishway in Hell's Gate. It was state-of-the-art technology at the time, but may never have worked as well as was believed. Nonetheless, since the fishway was built, sockeye stocks have been recovering in the Fraser. In 1993, some 22 million returned to the system. And bigger runs are anticipated in the years ahead. Some people have even begun to talk about a return to near-historical levels — with runs of 50 million sockeye now seen as possible.

But to expect sockeye runs to simply get larger is to lose sight of history. The fish can vanish again suddenly. Habitat damage, as the building of a dam on the Nechako River illustrates, is a constant threat. And so too is the danger of overfishing.

Every user group — commercial, sport, native — is constantly demanding a bigger slice of the salmon resource. The federal Department of Fisheries is caught in a delicate and dangerous balancing act, where it tries to weigh economic benefits against environmental considerations. What is good for the salmon is, of course, good for all the fishers in the long run. But when bills are due and the salmon are in, incredible pressures are placed on fisheries managers to increase the harvest.

There's a thriving native fishery in the Fraser Canyon. Pole gill-netting, shown here, is a traditional method for catching salmon.

Archie Charles, chief of the Seabird Island Band, at his drying station in Saddle Rock Canyon, east of Yale. The salmon are hung on racks to be dried by the winds coming up the canyon.

Stream feeding into the Fraser River.

*Yale, the end of the
Fraser Canyon. From
here the river flows
gently 200 kilometers to
the Strait of Georgia.*

Salmon smolts find safety from predators in the eelgrass of the estuary.

Heron in the Fraser estuary.

*Looking east to Vancouver over the
Fraser estuary. The estuary delta grows as
the Fraser deposits its load of silt.*

*OPPOSITE:
A westcoast seiner drums a good catch
of Adams sockeye on board.*

The silty water of the Fraser meets the blue waters of the Strait of Georgia. At some times of the year, the Fraser Plume extends more than six kilometers into the Strait.

Politicians frequently interfere, leaning on bureaucrats who in turn pressure field managers and scientists. Overfishing has immediate effects by reducing the number of spawners on the grounds — and over time it can have a cumulative impact that is devastating. Anyone who thinks that British Columbia's salmon stocks can't collapse the way East Coast cod stocks did during the late 1980s is in foolish denial.

It was politicized management of the fishery that led to problems in 1992, when nearly 483,000 Stuart sockeye disappeared from the Fraser River. The stock had already been overfished by the time it arrived, and the new aboriginal fishery had been launched so quickly it didn't have adequate checks in place.

One of the unexpected benefits of the "vanishing sockeye" controversy, however, was that late running stocks were able to pass upriver because the Lower Fraser was closed to fishing from August onwards. The Adams run, and the rare Thompson River steelhead, went through without loss. That fall 12,000 sockeye spawned in the Adams River — three times the number that had come back four years earlier and the highest for that chronically weak cycle in more than 40 years. Biologists also reported the biggest return of Thompson steelhead in decades, although it was still just a few thousand fish.

When bills are due and the salmon are in, incredible pressures are placed on fisheries managers to increase the harvest. Politicians frequently interfere, leaning on bureaucrats who in turn pressure field managers and scientists.

The emergency closure of the Fraser fishery in the summer of 1992 demonstrated convincingly that the best way to get fish on the spawning grounds and rebuild a run is to reduce fishing pressure.

Looking at the tragically low numbers of Adams fish that run on the 1992 cycle (716 spawners one year), it is hard to understand why more strategic closures aren't used. Since 1956, a total of only 42,773 sockeye have spawned in the Adams on all the low-cycle years put together. That's less than the number that usually spawns in a single year on the next weakest cycle, and just a fraction of the 2 million-plus

The tagging operation on the Adams. Sockeye are caught, tagged, and released. When recovered, these tags provide data for the management of the spawning grounds.

dominant-year runs. It's clear from what happened after the 1992 closure of the Fraser that fisheries managers have it in their power to restore both the low-cycle Adams run, and the endangered Thompson steelhead. If only they have the will.

Studies in 1993 found that nine of ten major salmon species were at risk of extinction across the U.S. Pacific Northwest. Overfishing and habitat destruction caused by logging and dam building were the main factors.

"Today we are at a crossroads — a point at which resource managers and the public must determine whether the Pacific salmon will recover or cease to exist in large segments of its range," an American group, the Wilderness Society, said in a report that provided the first comprehensive mapping of salmon habitat in Oregon, Washington, Idaho and California.

"Habitat loss and population declines have been so dramatic in this century that it now appears that wild salmon are only about 20 percent as abundant in the region as they were historically. It is likely that most populations will be permanently lost if current conditions persist or worsen," stated Mike Anderson, one of the report's authors.

Overfishing is no longer a problem in the U.S. Pacific Northwest — simply because most commercial fishing operations have gone out of business.

In British Columbia there remains a thriving commercial industry that involves 5,000 vessels, 15,000 workers and 7,000 shore-based workers. In addition there is a booming sports fishery, with high-volume fishing lodges now in operation all along the coast from the northern tip of the Queen Charlotte Islands to Barkley Sound on southern Vancouver Island. And there is a rapidly developing native commercial fishery in coastal rivers.

It has long been recognized that B.C.'s commercial fleet is too big for the resource. Now it's got competition from sports and native fisheries that are growing. But as yet no government has had the courage to tackle the problem of downsizing the fleet. So every season immense pressure is brought on the government to allow a greater harvest. At the same time, logging, dam building and industrial/urban development continue to erode salmon habitat.

Every fourth year the Adams run comes booming in, flooding the Strait of Georgia and the Fraser River with fish. Big catches on dominant runs suddenly swamp the market, depressing prices. The result is that even in dominant years, commercial fishers aren't getting enough fish to make the kind of money they need.

University of British Columbia fisheries scientists Carl Walters and Michael J. Staley drew some fascinating and important conclusions after they studied the cyclic dominance of Fraser River sockeye stocks.

"Cyclic abundances now appear to be maintained largely by high fishing rates," they wrote, "and it is possible that aboriginal fisheries were responsible for establishment of the cyclic patterns that have been inferred from historical records. By lowering exploitation rates on all stocks in all cycle years, it should be possible to substantially increase the value of the fishery even if some very weak off-cycle runs never recover."

SALMON AROUND THE WORLD?

Numerous attempts have been made to stock sockeye in other parts of the world, mostly without success. By as early as 1938 scientists had concluded there was nowhere that could support the fish in numbers comparable to the North Pacific.

The scientists argue for "giving up some catches in the short term in favor of substantially larger and more stable harvests in the long run."

If they are right, then by reducing the catch in weak cycle years, managers should be able to greatly boost the overall productivity of the Adams River. That would mean, however, cutting back on the catch during lean years, when commercial fishers can least afford it.

It's a tough balancing act. And it is sobering to recall that the Americans failed to maintain their balance and all but lost their salmon as a result. The same thing happened on the East Coast, where cod stocks have been destroyed, declining by 95 percent since 1990 and throwing 20,000 people out of work.

Are we smart enough to save our salmon? Do we care enough? Or are we just the same as the cod fishermen, who protested against every closure until, in the bitter end, there was nothing left to catch?

CHAPTER SEVEN

HOME

RIVER

We had stopped for lunch near where Hiuihill Creek enters the Adams River when the man came running up. His face was pale and he was short of breath. He was sweating. We looked up, wondering what on earth to expect, and then he blurted it out: "Bear!" He gestured back down the trail, swallowed and went on. "I saw a bear. It's been following me up the trail. You better get out of here." Then he was gone, hurrying back towards the car park. With two little kids in tow we thought it best not to hang around, and reluctantly followed him. The girls kept looking back over their shoulders, hoping to see the bear, but they never did.

In the fall, when the salmon return, about twenty black bears come down from the hills to feed on them. They are not interested in people. They want only the salmon. Sometimes they walk along the trails because, like humans, they find it easier going. What is probably most remarkable about the bears of the Adams River is that they interact so rarely with people. You see their footprints in the soft sand and mud along the river, but usually you don't see the bears. They like to feed at night, when the tourists have gone, and then they curl up and sleep in the underbrush during the day. It is something to think that, while crowds of people wander about, looking at the salmon, a small herd of bears is sleeping not far away, their bellies full of sockeye.

With an arch of the back and a flip of the tail, a sockeye digs a nest or redd.

It is interesting that the bears come back to the river before the salmon do. The eagles are the same. You can always tell the salmon are coming to a river by looking at the tree tops. The eagles will be there, waiting. I think the eagles know in advance because they see the salmon jumping in the lake as they approach the river. Or perhaps they are signalled by the activities of the ducks, mallards, green-winged teals and goldeneye, which are also attracted by the salmon. But the bears? I haven't figured that one out yet. Like the salmon themselves, they could be measuring the length of the days, or responding to genetic programming that tells them to return to the Adams in the fall.

You can see the salmon coming. They splash across Little Shuswap Lake, leave boils and swirls on the slick surface of Little River, then hold off the mouth of the Adams until they are ready to spawn. When the run starts, they come in successive waves, wriggling across the shallows at the river mouth.

It is impossible to know what the Adams smells like to them, but ever since they reached the Fraser Plume they have been searching for the scent of their home river. The olfactory nerve inside their nostril cavity helped them find the Fraser, then it led them into the clear waters of the Thompson and back to Shuswap Lake.

Sockeye sometimes stray to new rivers. That is how the nearby Salmon River got recruits after its huge run of summer sockeye went extinct in the river in 1913. Now it has a small number of fall-run sockeye. Fish that branch out into new water are called pioneers, and over the centuries have played a vital role in extending the range of sockeye and other salmon species. But it has been estimated that fully 97 percent of the salmon that make it back from the ocean — and past the fishing nets — return to their home river. A mere 3 percent go wandering, and that usually only happens on dominant years when the spawning beds are crowded.

By the time the sockeye return to the Shuswap they are in full spawning colors, with vibrant red bodies and green heads. The males have been transformed, developing pronounced humps, displaying large spawning teeth, and getting a dramatic hook — known as a kype — to their upper jaws. The skin of both sexes undergoes a remarkable change as a pigment in the cells turns the fish red. The transformation is caused by the release of sex hormones, apparently triggered by the pineal gland which measures light.

The vivid colors serve as a visual stimulant to other fish and signal readiness to spawn. (The intensification of carotinoid pigment in the skin also makes it easier for the fish to take in oxygen, which is important on the spawning grounds.) The misshapen jaws, the oversize teeth and the humped back are all used by the males for displays of power. The hump may also be what makes the males a preferred target for bears. In an Alaska study of sockeye it was found that the bears predominantly took males. One look at sockeye coming up through a shallow run and you'll know why — the hump sticks out like a flag.

As is typical of territorial males, whether they be fish, animal or bird, a lot of the activity that leads up to spawning is built on intimidation. With their big humped backs and bluff charges, the male sockeye try to assert themselves. Fish threaten

Fish that branch out into new water are called pioneers, and over the centuries have played a vital role in extending the range of sockeye and other salmon species.

On the spawning beds, sockeye pair off in anticipation of mating.

intruders by displaying their mouth lining, spreading their fins or by making a direct threatening approach. Butting and biting can follow. One technique used by salmon is to grab the opponent by the narrow part of the body, commonly called the wrist, just in front of the tail. The attacker then twists violently. The kype of a salmon, with its arcing shape and large teeth, is a fearsome weapon. Getting a good tail twist is usually enough to drive off an interloper.

Big males usually mate with big females, chasing away the smaller competitors. The big females in turn have used their size to assert their claim to the best spawning gravel. Smaller males, who are usually less aggressive and who wander about the spawning grounds more, will take up satellite positions around the dominant males if they can't find mates of their own. This can lead to fighting. But if they are patient, the smaller males may get a chance to mate when the dominant males weaken and die. The females will stay over the redd for several days, and may spawn again with a second male if they have any eggs left. But studies of pink and chum salmon suggest that many small males simply don't get to spawn much. At death the smaller males were found to have retained large quantities of unused sperm. It may be that the small males are nature's way of ensuring a back-up system.

Only females build nests. Males may appear at times to be nest building, but they are mimicking the females for reasons that biologists don't understand. A male who is digging will usually move a meter or so away from the female so his activity does not interfere with hers. It may be that the male is sending a signal to the female, trying to stimulate her into spawning. In one test a group of female sockeye was isolated from males. Without the visual stimulus of males, with their distinctive humped backs and jaws, it took the females several days longer to build their nests and lay eggs.

At first glance a salmon nest seems a crude affair. It is simply a hole scooped out in the gravel. But the female puts a lot of work into constructing it. Water flow, temperature, and the quality of the substrate, or river bottom, are all factors instinctively weighed by the fish in choosing a site.

Before digging, a female moves slowly over the gravel, feeling the substrate with her body and fins. When she has found a place to her liking, she turns on her side and, with a violent arcing movement, thrashes several times towards the rocks. Often her tail will not actually strike the bottom; the downward force of water is enough to dislodge sediment and small stones, which wash away with the current. Larger rocks tumble back into the cavity, creating deep crevasses that will later be used as hiding places by emerging alevins. After a few seconds she drifts downstream to rest, then moves up and repeats the process. This time she uses her other flank to strike at the gravel. Alternating from one side to the next she will dig several times before the nest is ready.

A sockeye's nest is on average 102 centimeters long and 85 centimeters wide. In slow water it will be more circular in shape; in faster water it will be oblong, trailing off to the downstream end. The hole will be about 9 centimeters deep and is made in such a manner that a small back eddy is created immediately in front of the nest, creating a downward flow that helps hold the eggs in place. The eggs are slightly adhesive when they are extruded, and will stick to the gravel for about twenty minutes. If they are not covered soon after spawning, they will be washed away.

Often the male sockeye will sidle up beside a female, touching her gently, and then his entire body will quiver. It is thought that hormonal secretions, perhaps by both the male and female, work as an olfactory stimulant.

The male stimulates the female into spawning not just by false nest building, but also by engaging in a form of courtship. His behavior and positioning, the way he attends constantly to her, chasing away intruders and brushing against her, are all signals that he is ready to spawn. Often a male will sidle up beside a female, touching her gently, and then his entire body will quiver. It is thought that hormonal secretions, perhaps by both the male and female, work as an olfactory stimulant. And surely the river, once spawning has begun, must carry a scent that is overwhelming to a salmon's powerful sense of smell. At peak spawning, as fluid extruded with the eggs and clouds of milt drift with the current, the river is a hormonal soup.

As they prepare to spawn, the salmon lower their tails into the nest, with the male at a slight angle to the female. When they are both ready, their mouths gape widely.

The eggs are laid in a burst, with several hundred deposited in each nest, but they do not come out lumped together. The skein, a sack which holds the eggs in the salmon's body, is a silky smooth membrane to which each egg is attached individually. Rather than being held like a loose bunch of marbles in a bag, the eggs are cupped like pomegranate seeds, each in its own concave cradle within the shell of the fish. These beautiful, delicate creations contain oil and enough nutrients to feed a developing salmon for several weeks. They also contain a germinal disk that is waiting to be triggered.

As she lays her eggs the male simultaneously jettisons his milt, sending a milky cloud over the nest. The current and the fanning movement of the tails swirls the sperm, inactive until it comes in contact with water, down into the depression. And the eggs, which swell rapidly when they are exposed to water, seal themselves the instant the outer membrane is penetrated by a single sperm. When eggs are fertilized in a bucket at a fish hatchery, it only takes a few drops of seminal fluid to fertilize hundreds of eggs. In the wild, spawning salmon release such a heavy concentration — about 50 million sperms in each spawning — that a white plume of surplus fluid can be seen drifting several feet downstream of the nest. The sperm stays alive for a few seconds to a few minutes, so the strategy is to overwhelm the nest area, ensuring total coverage of the eggs.

Hidden in the protective gravel of the redd, the eggs and alevins are safe from such predators as trout.

Immediately after the spawning act, which lasts less than twenty seconds and often takes place at night, the female moves above the nest and soon begins to dig again. This time she moves at a more frantic pace as she works to cover her eggs, to stop them from drifting away and to protect them from predators. Some sockeye

With a violent upswing of her tail, a female dislodges gravel that is swept downstream by the current. She builds a shallow nest while a male stands guard nearby.

have been observed digging as many as 27 times in a five-minute period, working with a clear sense of urgency. Half an hour after spawning she starts to build a new nest, usually just upstream. Much of the material she digs this time will drift down with the current and add to the covering on her earlier nest. Eventually she will build several nests, depositing a few thousand eggs. The collection of nests is known as a redd.

In the Adams River on a dominant run, every square meter of gravel in some of the pools will be used. There are only about 60 hectares of usable gravel in the river, which means there might be 20,000 salmon per hectare during a big run. By some estimates it is the most valuable real estate in the province, producing hundreds of millions of dollars worth of salmon yearly.

Sockeye concentrate in the prime areas, particularly in the lower two kilometers of river between the highway bridge and the lake, where 62 percent of the sockeye spawn. About 38 percent of the run spawns in the 9.6 kilometers above the bridge, most intensely in side channels. There is some debate over how much salmon disturb other redds when they are nest building. Some observers believe if too many fish get on the beds they will destroy existing nests. But others say the salmon seem to have an instinctive sense about where nests are located, and most will seek out fresh gravel.

The two main tributaries of the Adams — Nikwikwaia (Gold) Creek and Hiuihill (Bear) Creek — support small runs of salmon. In 1991, with 1.2 million sockeye in the main river, there were just 615 spawners in Hiuihill Creek and 2,000 in Nikwikwaia.

The flow of the Adams in October has had dramatic variations over the decades, ranging from a low of 15.9 cubic meters per second (cms) in 1916, to a high of 109 cms in 1959. Mostly, however, the river is somewhere between 30 and 50 cms, with a mean of 49.6 cms. It is probably more than coincidence that the low water year of 1916 matches up with the weakest cycle in the Adams. Low water means there are fewer places for salmon to spawn, less oxygen for the incubating eggs, and less protection for the nests from gouging by ice.

T he spawning period shifts slightly from year to year, but the second week in October is generally considered the peak. In 1991 the bulk of the spawning took place from October 15 to 28 and the following year it was October 3 to 10.

The timing of the spawning cycle is critical because it, together with water temperatures over the winter, determines when the young salmon will be launched into the world. Their arrival in the spring must coincide with the plankton blooms in the lake, and a year later, their outmigration must coincide with plankton blooms in the Strait of Georgia. The key environmental cues that trigger the salmon are light and temperature. There are probably other factors that are measured by the fish in ways that we do not understand, but those are the two main factors.

Whatever the triggers are, it is clear the whole life cycle is so precisely timed it's as if the spawners are finely meshed gears in a cosmic clock.

So what would happen if the temperature of the Adams River was changed? Could the sockeye become uncoupled from the sequence of events that has been their key to survival for thousands of years?

Two British Columbia scientists looked at that very question and came up with a disturbing answer. Michael Henderson and John Stockner wanted to know what the consequences of global warming would be on the Adams River.

Global warming, brought on by the accumulation of greenhouse gases such as carbon dioxide in the atmosphere, is expected to result in increased temperature and changes to precipitation patterns throughout North America.

OTHER BIG RUNS

Spawning salmon can be seen in over 1,300 rivers and streams in B.C. The Horsefly River, near Quesnel, has a sockeye run that rivals the Adams in size; it peaks August 25 to September 5. The Raft River, in the North Thompson district, peaks at the same date. The Vedder River (Chilliwack), Seton Creek (Lillooet), and the Coquihalla (Hope) have pink runs in mid-October. The Cheakamus River (Squamish) has a chum run from mid-November, as does the Big Qualicum (Qualicum Beach) on Vancouver Island.

Viewing stations have been built along the Adams River to assist the public in watching the sockeye.

Henderson and Stockner say air temperatures in the vicinity of the Adams will probably increase by 4°Celsius in the summer and 2.5°C in the winter. The temperature change will alter the production characteristics of the lake, reducing the availability of food for juvenile sockeye, decreasing growth rates and leading to reduced survival in fresh and salt water.

With warmer summers and less severe winters, the spring runoff that now dominates the hydrology of the lake will be flattened out. More nutrients will be flushed into the lake during the winter, at a time when light and temperature won't be ideal for plankton production. The result would be a shift in the structure of the plankton populations from larger to smaller organisms. That means the fish would have to work harder to get their food.

"It appears that the thermal niche of juvenile sockeye salmon is becoming uncoupled from their feeding niche in Shuswap Lake," warn Henderson and Stockner.

"Overall, we think large, interior systems like Shuswap Lake will . . . become increasingly similar to coastal systems which have been shown to be considerably less productive and to produce smaller juvenile sockeye salmon."

The Adams River is already starting to warm up. From 1959 to 1989 the average temperature has increased from 10°C to 11.5°C. Studies on other Fraser systems indicate the optimum spawning temperature for sockeye is in the range of 13°C to 15°C, which suggests the Adams will still be ideal spawning habitat even if the water temperature increases a few degrees because of global warming. But a four-degree jump, which is predicted in the next century, will push the temperature over the threshold.

Adams River sockeye are near the southern extreme for the species in North America. It is believed the boundary is determined more by temperature than by anything else. With increases in temperature, the boundary could be pushed north — leading to substantial declines in the Adams run.

Among other things, warmer river water could affect the development of the embryos, possibly speeding up the date of emergence and putting the fry into the lake earlier in the spring — before the prime plankton bloom. The impact could be devastating.

Henderson and Stockner say they are "reasonably certain" there will be an overall decline of sockeye production.

"This conclusion is based on two lines of evidence. Temperature is probably the most important environmental determinant of sockeye salmon life history. Further, sockeye salmon have adapted to synchronizing events in their life history with the temperature regimes of the rivers and lakes they encounter. As a result, most of the behavioral, and ecological traits exhibited are genetically encoded, and stock specific. The rapid increase in temperature anticipated over the next 50 to 150 years will almost certainly exceed the ability of Adams River sockeye salmon to respond on a genetic basis, and as a result, lead to a decrease in growth and survival."

The Adams River is a perfect salmon stream right now. You can sense that when you walk along its banks. Even in the heat of summer it's so cool you need a sweater under the forest canopy that shades the water's edge. The soil is damp. When it rains the mountains slowly feed the streams that rush to life and pour oxygen into the lakes and river. In the spring there are blossoms everywhere, pink and yellow and orange. There are five species of orchids and 125 different types of plants, including Oregon grape, California filbert, creambush oceanspray and chokecherry. There is poverty oatgrass, rough-fruited fairy-bells, racemouse pussytoes and pipe cleaner moss. There are bats, toads, otters, beaver, mule deer, eagles, ospreys, coyotes and bears.

There are places along the trail where you will see the remains of winter houses, the rectangular depressions softened by thick grass with trees eighteen meters high springing from the ruins. And there are pictographs, slowly vanishing under blankets of ancient lichens.

In October you can catch the scent of the river, rich with the death of salmon. It smells like the sea and it is wonderful.

SOURCES

This book would not have been possible without the help of a great many people. We would like to thank the scientists, biologists and native elders who shared their knowledge with us, in particular Dr. John Stockner for explaining the intricacies of the minute world of picoplankton.

We are greatly indebted to Darwin and Susan Baerg, of Fraser River Raft Expeditions in Yale, for guiding us safely through the Fraser Canyon, and to Neil Todd and Jackie Stibbards of Diversified OvaTech for allowing photographic access to the salmon at Spious Creek Hatchery. Dr. Don Pepper at BCIT kindly generated the graphs illustrating salmon frequencies. Alex Rose provided great inspiration in starting the whole project.

Don and Nora Munro of Salmon Arm were gracious hosts for many field trips to the Adams River, and use of the Butters family cabin on Little Shuswap Lake was also greatly appreciated.

To Troutman — thanks for the Little River, at dusk, when the bats were flying.

Finally, we would like to thank our families for nurturing our interest in rivers.

Following are some of the materials used in researching this book:

Beamish, Richard J. and Daniel R. Bouillon. "Pacific Salmon Production Trends in Relation to Climate." *Canadian Journal of Fisheries and Aquatic Sciences*, vol. 50 no. 5, 1993.

Bond, Carl E. *Biology of Fishes*. W.B. Saunders Co., 1979.

Brown, Bill and Greta Lundborg. *Archaeological Resources of the Lower Adams River*. Provincial Archaeologist's Office, Heritage Conservation Branch, Government of British Columbia, 1977.

Burgner, Robert L. "Some Features of Ocean Migrations and Timing of Pacific Salmon." In McNeil, W.J. *Salmonid Ecosystems of the North Pacific*.

Chebanov, N.A. "Materials on the Assortive Crossing and the Role of Sex Ratio during the Spawning Period of the Pacific Salmons." In McNeil, W.J. *Salmonid Ecosystems of the North Pacific*.

Coffey, J. and E. Goldstrom, G. Gottfriedson, R. Matthew, and P. Walton. *Shuswap History: The First 100 Years of Contact*. Secwepemc Cultural Education Society.

Cooperman, Jim and Mary Zoretich, editors. *Shuswap Chronicles*, vol. II, 1989.

Duff, Wilson. *The Upper Stalo Indians of the Fraser River of B.C.* Anthropology Memoir #1, B.C. Provincial Museum, 1952.

Foerster, Russell E. *The Sockeye Salmon.* Fisheries Research Board of Canada, Bulletin 162, 1968.

Groot, Cornelis and Leo Margolis. *Pacific Salmon Life Histories.* UBC Press, 1991.

Healey, M.C. "The Ecology of Juvenile Salmon in Georgia Strait, British Columbia."

Henderson, Michael A. and John G. Stockner. "Probable Consequences of Climate Change on Freshwater Production of Adams River Sockeye Salmon." *GeoJournal,* September 1992.

Krogius, F.V. "The Growth of Young Sockeye of Different Year Classes and Fluctuations in Primary Production in Lake Dalneye. Abstracts of Soviet Salmonid Studies." In McNeil, W.J. *Salmonid Ecosystems of the North Pacific.*

McNeil, William J. and Daniel C. Himsworth, editors. *Salmonid Ecosystems of the North Pacific.* Oregon State University Press and Oregon State University Sea Grant College Program, 1980.

Mohs, Gordon. *An Assessment and Evaluation of Heritage Resources in the South Thompson River Valley of British Columbia.* Occasional papers, Heritage Conservation Branch, Government of British Columbia.

Pearcy, William G. *Ocean Ecology of North Pacific Salmonids.* University of Washington Press, 1992.

Peterman, Randall M. "Testing for Density-Dependent Marine Survival in Pacific Salmonids."

Roos, John F. *Restoring Fraser River Salmon.* The Pacific Salmon Commission.

Sanger, David. *The Chase Burial Site, British Columbia.* Bulletin 224, National Museums of Canada.

Smith, H.D., L. Margolis and C.C. Wood. *Sockeye Salmon Population Future Management.* Department of Fisheries and Oceans, 1985.

Stockner, John G. "Autotrophic Picoplankton in Freshwater Ecosystems." *Internationale Revue der gesamten Hydrobiologie,* 1991.

————. *Lake Fertilization: The Enrichment Cycle and Lake Sockeye Salmon Production.* Canadian Special Publication of Fisheries and Aquatic Sciences 96, 1987.

Stockner, John G. and Naval J. Antia. "Algal Picoplankton from Marine and Freshwater Ecosystems: A Multidisciplinary Perspective." *Can. J. Fish. Aquatic Science,* 1986.

Stockner, John G. and K.D. Hyatt. "Lake Fertilization: State of the Art after Seven Years of Application." *Canadian Technical Report of Fisheries and Aquatic Sciences #1324,* 1984.

Stockner, John G. and K.S. Shortreed. *Autotrophic Picoplankton: Community Composition, Abundance and Distribution across a Gradient of Oligotrophic British Columbia and Yukon Territory Lakes.* Department of Fisheries and Oceans, 1991.

Walters, Carl J. and Michael J. Staley. "Evidence Against the Existence of Cyclic Dominance in Fraser River Sockeye Salmon."

Weber, Lavern J. and John R. Smith. "Possible Role of the Pineal Gland in Migratory Behaviour of Salmonids." In McNeil, W.J. *Salmonid Ecosystems of the North Pacific.*

INDEX

Mark Hume is a senior reporter for the Vancouver *Sun* where he has covered stories relating to fisheries and the environment. He is the author of *The Run of the River*.

Rick Blacklaws specializes in the photographic illustration of Western Canada's natural and cultural history. His work has been featured in numerous books and magazines. He currently teaches at Langara College.

Tom Moore is the owner/designer of Moore Davies Graphics. For the past five years he has worked to develop new ways of imparting information in graphics and illustrations.